HOW D

IS

MY VALLEY

A record of the gross abuse of the mining communities in the Dearne Valley of South Yorkshire by aristocrats, the establishment and governments. Miners and their families were considered to be semi-barbarous, a people apart and an inferior race. Many will say nothing has changed.

Peter Hargreaves

ISBN: 978-1-291-43877-2

www.publishnation.co.uk

EXPLANATION....

I previously authored a local history of the Dearne Valley (The Place of Wells) with the intention of self-publishing sufficient copies to distribute to local libraries and organisations. However, since then I have had many requests to republish and make further copies for sale to the general public.

I've taken the opportunity to extend the story line and also to indulge in some autobiographical detail which I hope will make my latest effort, "How Dark is my Valley", even more interesting.

For those readers who had the opportunity to read 'The Place of the Wells', I hope you will find my latest effort even more interesting and an accurate reflection on the life, politics and suffering to which the people of the Valley have been subjected over many years.

This book is dedicated to my late parents Fred and Rose Hargreaves whose love and dedication to their children helped us survive all the years of misery, political strife and economic suffering in the Valley. Their memory will stay with us forever. Two deeply loved parents. Now at peace.

What you will read in this book....

Page

1 M Valley
4 Early history
6 Coal mining in the Valley
8 Criminal working conditions
10 The spirit of revolt
11 Pit explosions in the Valley
12 The Lundhill pit disaster
15 After the disaster
16 The Barnsley Old Oaks pit disaster
17 The miners' strike of 1893
21 Valley men and the Boer War
23 The miners' struggle....the Liberal Party....
and the birth of the Labour Party....
27 From relative peace....then dragged into war
27 War is declared
29 The Valley went to war
31 The battle for 'Serre' the Somme...1st July 1916....
'THE PALS' 13 & 14th Battalions the York and Lancs
36 The attack
39 After the attack
41 After the war....almost revolution
43 From one war to the next
46 Life in the Valley between the wars
49 World War Two
49 The cost of war
50 The Home Guard
50 Growing-up during World War Two
52 Toys in wartime
53 Christmas day during the war
54 War-time rationing
57 The Barnsley British Co-operative Society
59 My heritage

60 Slums, outside toilets, bed bugs and chamber pots
63 Bathing, cooking and gas light
65 Household duties
67 Home entertainment
70 Seaside trips
72 Cinemas and roller-rinks
73 Street gangs
75 The canal-bank
77 Churches, Chapels and The Salvation Army
79 The National Health Service
80 Chemist shops
80 Education in the Valley
86 Houghton Main Colliery
93 National Service
97 Return to the Valley
99 Lipton Limited
102 Politics and Wombwell Urban District Council
106 The 1972 miners' strike and the rise of Arthur Scargill
108 Peace in the Valley but not for long
110 Prime Minister Margaret Thatcher
112 1984....into the strike
116 Betrayal
117 Beaten....but defiant
117 After the strike
118 Thatcher planned revenge on the miners
120 If Scargill had beaten Thatcher
122 After Thatcher
123 Labour Party history repeats itself
125 My Valley
125 The author
128 Also by the author

My Valley....

....is the Dearne Valley, and my home is the small former mining town of Wombwell situated in the heart of the Dearne Valley, South Yorkshire; with Barnsley to the north and Rotherham to the south. With the development of substantial road infrastructure, motorists passing through South Yorkshire would be unlikely to pass through the once bubbling towns of Barnsley, Wombwell, Darfield, Wath, Mexborough and Conisborough. It was the coal mining towns in the Valley where the mythical weighing of Labour Party votes originated.

The Dearne Valley is not accorded much of national history and is mostly remembered as the place where coal was mined; where the people speak a strange language and was the stomping ground for Arthur Scargill and the extreme left-wing of the National Union of Mineworkers. Factually however, it has a rich history going back to early Saxon times when in 65 the Romans invaded Yorkshire. Saxon resistance was so strong it took the hugely superior Roman army over five years to subdue the local tribes. Prior to the arrival of the Romans the Saxons had been locked in continuous battles with Vikings raiding and plundering from the north. After the Romans eventually gave-up trying to subdue the Saxons and beat off repeated attacks by the Vikings, they withdrew their legions and concentrated their armies in Europe. But Britain had to suffer another invasion when the Normans decided Britain was worth conquering. After the Norman King William defeated King Harold at the battle of Hastings and succeeded in subduing the northern tribes; he was successful in establishing law and order in Britain, even though stoutly resisted, and at the price of imposing on England a dynasty of foreign monarchs and aristocrats.

More recent history that had a big impact on the Valley was unquestionably the industrial revolution that precipitated the building of canals and railways to support the local coal producing and steel making industries. The history of the coal mining industry in the

Valley is either good or bad depending on which aspect is considered. Although industrial development blighted the environment and natural beauty of the Valley, it did however provide thousands of jobs for the unemployed across England and Wales and helped to sustain many impoverished families. It was also an unmitigated disaster that destroyed the fabric of a peasant society.

The frantic rush to mine coal to meet the insatiable demands of vast new industries created an unregulated mining industry which resulted in many underground explosions such as those at the Lundhill Colliery Wombwell and the Oaks Colliery Barnsley that devastated whole communities. However, disgraceful and often inhumane working conditions spawned the early miners' unions and eventually the National Union of Mineworkers that helped to build the Labour Party to become the catalyst for reform in the treatment and welfare of the working-class.

In spite of the many injustices inflicted by uncaring governments and employers, the mining communities stayed patriotic, so that when Lord Kitchener made the call for volunteers to fight against Germany at the outbreak of the First World War, thousands of miners from the Valley trooped into the recruiting office at Barnsley to volunteer. Regrettably it is another part of the Valley's history that a seemingly uncaring Monarch, Prime Minister and incompetent generals were prepared to squander needlessly the lives of miners; resulting in thousands of widows, fatherless children and grief stricken communities.

Sadly, after the war to end all wars little changed for the miners. Social conditions and the treatment of miners worsened and brought about the 1926 miners' strike that lasted over a year with many families surviving only with the aid of soup kitchens and food distributed by charities.

Although they were still treated very badly for many years after the strike, the miners again responded to the nation's call to arms when in 1939 war erupted a second time with Germany. Although thousands of citizens from the Valley were drafted into the armed forces; this time the most urgent need was for the miners from the Valley to produce the huge amounts of coal required to produce power for massive new arms factories needed to supply an army, navy and air-force that was in action continuously for six years, as well as keeping the home fires burning. Although it was the military men and women who fought the battles, defended Britain and won the war, it could not have been achieved without the dedicated contribution from Britain's coal miners.

After the end of the war in Europe in 1945 and to much surprise, Winston Churchill was rejected as Prime Minister at the general-election after the nation voted overwhelmingly for a Labour government. One of the new Prime Minister Clement Atlee's first major acts was to nationalise the coal mining industry; taking it out of private ownership and placing it under the control of the government. The act ensured that for the first time miners would be employed in safer working conditions and paid fair wages for their labour.

However, after changes in government the miners again had to struggle when Tory governments were elected. After the bitter defeat of Edward Heath's Tory government by the miners, the next Tory government under Margaret Thatcher decided the nation would be better off without continuous disruptions to the power supply by striking miners, and further, no longer needed a mining industry as new oil and gas discoveries flowed from the North Sea. Margaret Thatcher then instituted a brutal pit closure programme in the early 1980's that totally devastated the mining communities, throwing thousands of miners out of work and onto the dole; creating such bitterness against the Tories that may never go away. Thirty years later, some of the younger miners from the 1980's are still unemployed with many condemned to spend the rest of their lives existing on government benefits. My Valley had been deeply scarred and may never recover from the disgraceful political decision that caused serious social decline in Britain's coal fields and caused consequences for the Tory Party from which it may never recover.

Although young men from the Valley leaving school no longer follow their fathers in working down the mines, there are few job opportunities and high unemployment has created social conditions that should be unacceptable to the British nation. It's a strange fact that with the demise of the mining industry, the Valley is starting to regain the natural beauty that made it so popular with the Romans and Normans and an environment for the Valley to be proud of. But the sad fact remains, that if Margaret Thatcher's government had had any consideration for the immense social tragedy they were creating, they would have planned for the aftermath of their destruction of the mining industry and the abandonment of the mining communities. It would seem that after Winston Churchill declared 'the miners were the enemy', they will always be regarded as such by the Tories, even if a defeated and demoralised enemy.

Early history....

The Dearne Valley was regarded by the Romans as one of the more pleasant places in the British Isles. A special attraction for them was the many wells, around which they were able to create bath houses to rest, relax and socialise in much the same way as they did in Rome. The abundance of many species of game and bird life provided an extra attraction for the homesick soldiery to exercise their hunting skills. The Valley became something of a holiday resort, not only for the soldiers, but also for the many government officials and their families who accompanied them on their long tours of duty overseas; subsequently the Valley became known as the 'Place of the Wells'.

The Romans were not alone in finding the Valley an attractive area as Vikings also settled permanently in some parts. Norman nobility also staked their claim early in the 'Conquest'. William, the first Earl of Warrene and son-in-law of King William I (The Conqueror) was given the 'Honour of Conisborough' by King William for his services in the conquest of England in 1066. The present remains of Conisborough Castle are not the original castle built by Earl Warenne in 1070. After several changes of ownership among his descendants, the stone 'Keep' of the castle as it now stands and additional buildings were built sometime after 1163. The castle must have rated highly at the time as King John I is known to have stayed there in 1201.

After numerous changes of ownership through the years, the castle fell into disrepair and the remains were granted to the Covey family by King Henry VIII. It was eventually bought by the local Conisborough council in the 1940's and is now in the care of English Heritage. Scott's 'Ivanhoe' was based around the castle.

Norman Lords De-Wombwell and Fitzwilliam were responsible for most of the early developments in the Valley. The De-Wombwell's were the occupiers of Wombwell Hall in Park Street Wombwell while the Fitzwilliam's were the owners of the huge Wentworth Woodhouse estate. The two aristocrats became the biggest landowners in the area. Later as owners of several of the biggest coal mines they were responsible for much of the degradation in the Valley.

My home town of Wombwell no longer appears on most road maps of England, even though it is mentioned in the Domesday Book of 1083. The Valley was not considered to have any importance in the region until a 1793 Act of Parliament allowed the construction of the Dearne and Dove canal. Chief shareholders were the Duke of Leeds, Earl Fitzwilliam and Sir George Wombwell. The canal opened previously inaccessible routes for delivering coal to Rotherham, Sheffield, Wakefield, Leeds and Manchester and took eleven years to complete.

The construction of the canal was no act of benevolence by the three aristocrats as it was built solely for their profit and the transporting of coal from their coal mines across the region; feeding the steel mills in Sheffield and Rotherham, providing fuel for industry in Lancashire and the steamships sailing in and out of the Manchester ship canal. The industrial revolution was entirely dependent on the supply of coal and the Valley became one of the major suppliers.

Although the development of the coal mining industry made fortunes for the aristocrats and many other wealthy landowners, it did little for the miners who had to claw the coal from a reluctant and often cruel mother-nature. If the Fitzwilliam's, De-Wombwell's and others left a legacy of their stewardship of the Valley, it was the treatment of the miners and their families that historically were some of the most horrific ever inflicted on a British social group and remain a stain on the reputation of aristocratic families, wealthy landowners and government.

Coal mining in the Valley....

The rush to mine coal to meet the huge industrial demand was ruthless and haphazard. Few men had been trained in the mining and engineering skills necessary for the successful extraction of coal from underground. Coal was found at various depths and some mines such as the Dearne Valley mine at Houghton could be extracted by drift mining (without having to sink a shaft down to the seam). But the best quality seams of coal that fetched the highest prices were found at deeper levels to which shafts had to be dug. Some seams were as deep as 220 yards and even more, but the extraction from deep seams was more difficult and extremely dangerous as the ever presence of gas was always a threat to the lives of miners.

Mine owners gave little consideration to the skills and equipment required for successful coal mining, and cared even less for the lives and welfare of their employees. Development of the industry was so fast and so vital to Britain's new industries that the government had little knowledge about the horrific working conditions imposed on the miners by greedy mine owners.

The biggest mines in the Valley were mostly owned by aristocrats and gentlemen land owners who employed agents to manage their mines, although there were other small mines operated by local entrepreneurs. Mine owners cared little how the agents operated so long as the profits continued to flow. Initially, many mine owners refused to buy ventilation equipment, essential in preventing gas explosions and protecting the health of miners exposed to fatal lung diseases because it was too expensive to buy and would reduce their profits.

There were eight large collieries in my area of the Valley. As new mines opened, many small villages in the vicinity quickly grew into townships as labour was imported to support the mines. However, the new townships developed without adequate planning and essential infrastructure to support the population explosion.

In my home town in the Valley, Wombwell Main colliery was the first large coalmine to be sunk in 1853 followed by Lundhill Colliery in1855, Darfield Main in 1860 and Mitchell's Main in 1870. As can be seen from the population figures for Wombwell, the population growth followed the opening of new mines:-

Population of Wombwell:
1801............614
1901........3 252
1961......18 777
1971......25 304

Although the building of the Dearne and Dove canal was the first major development in the Valley, another key development was the construction of the South Yorkshire Railway between Barnsley and Doncaster in 1857 and later between Barnsley and Sheffield, connecting a vital link from the coal fields to the big steel industries and eventually providing passenger services.

As the mining industry continued to grow, the Valley soon became littered with unsightly spoil heaps and acres of colliery sites with huge winding wheels topping pit shafts and standing like statues peering down over a forlorn mess. Where once had been rustic villages, these had given way to rows and rows of terrace slums that grew all too quickly into slum townships.

The biggest ever people migration to take place in Britain began as masses of unemployed and impoverished people from all over the British Isles migrated to the coal-fields seeking employment. Some mines could employ as many as three hundred men, who with their families had to be accommodated, but as cheaply as possible. To achieve this mine-owner's built long rows of small two bedroom houses with a kitchen and a small living room. Bedrooms were tiny but had to suffice for usually large families. Candlelight was the only lighting and the only facilities were a stone sink and a coal cooking range; water had to be carried in. Toilets (long drop) were built near the houses and had to be shared with several families. Some of the toilets were still in use well into the 1970's

Traders set up shops in the new communities and exploited the miners mercilessly as the miners had few alternatives in choosing where to buy. They also had to buy their own working tools so employers opened (tommy shops) to sell miners picks, shovels and even candles and matches that were usually the cause of gas explosions underground. Ale houses did big business as miners needed to quench their thirst after working long shifts in suffocating heat and clouds of coal dust; while others needed the solace of ale to cloud the pain of their miserable existence.

Criminal working conditions....

Miners in the Valley in the 19thCentury were held in very low regard and were described as reckless, semi-barbarous and as living more like savages than human beings; a people apart and an inferior race. Strong words; however it is doubtful if any of the critics who were around in the 1860's, would have been aware of the appalling degradation and inhumane working and living conditions to which miners and their families were subjected.

Men were mostly employed in the digging of coal and often had to work in seams barely wide enough to crawl through. Women and children (boys and girls some as young as six years-of-age) were employed but were paid considerably less than men; some were only there to assist their fathers to produce his required quota. Work underground was extremely dangerous and more so for young children, many of whom died in accidents and who were compelled to work long hours, sometimes as long as twelve hours a-day. This seriously affected their physical development causing some to become bow-legged and stunted in growth.

Many of the miners' children succumbed easily to disease; their bodies weakened through malnutrition had no resistance against scarlet fever, diphtheria and tuberculosis. There was little education for the children and most grew-up illiterate, preventing them from obtaining jobs outside the mines. It was reported that moral standards among miners' children were low and few had any understanding of the Bible or religion.

Conditions down most mines were extremely hot, so much so that men and boys often worked completely naked, while women and girls would work naked to the waist. Women employed were mostly young as most women were already starting to bear children by the age of sixteen. The unhealthy moral situation of young women working with naked men resulted in many being sexually abused, or in some cases the more enterprising women used their time underground to boost their earnings selling sexual services to the higher paid miners at the coal face. It's believed some women went underground without management knowledge to sell their services.

Many thousands of men, women and children died in Britain's coal mines in the rush to fuel the industrial revolution. As the demand for coal increased, deeper shafts had to be sunk to reach the wider and more profitable seams. As the industry expanded the number of mine disasters increased but there was little concern from government. The lives of miners were cheap and there were always many others waiting and eager to take their place.

Families of miners killed in accidents or disabled through industrial disease were usually thrown out of company owned housing to make way for replacement miners and their families. When they couldn't afford to pay rent elsewhere and became destitute, women had to settle for re-marriage, welcome or not, or face the dreaded workhouse. Medical facilities available to the mining communities were few, resulting in the deaths of many children at an early age. Miners contracting lung disease as a result of years inhaling coal dust were left to die agonising and lingering deaths. Burials were too expensive and relatives had to settle for seeing their loved ones and even little children buried in unmarked graves, around and close to, but not always in an often unwelcome church cemetery.

Some religious organisations such as The Salvation Army and the Wesleyans battled to bring relief to the mining communities, but their resources were few and they could do little more than offer spiritual comfort. The Churches and Chapels were mostly for the upper and middle class, while the heathens in the miners' cabins were left rejected and spiritually neglected.

The spirit of revolt....

Working conditions and continuous cuts in miners' wages in the Valley became so bad that the miners started to organise into trade unions, even though previous attempts had failed due to powerful and influential mine-owners who had the backing of civil authorities who did not hesitate to use their power and authority against the miners, including the use of the military.

Serious conflicts would erupt when the market price of coal dropped due to fluctuations in supply and demand. Mine owners would respond by cutting miners' wages to protect their profits, even though in good times miners barely earned enough to feed their families. Unions would call for strikes against cuts in wages, but mine-owners would respond by dismissing them for striking and then used the civil-authorities to evict them from their houses; throwing their families and possessions onto the streets.

In spite of ruthless treatment by the mine-owners and almost total absence of resources to help those victimised, communities rallied round their distressed comrades and helped to support them through to better times; even sharing already overcrowded accommodation. Gradually a new spirit and determination to survive started to grow.

Pit explosions in my Valley....

My home for many years and prior to leaving for South Africa in 1980 was in Lundhill Road Wombwell, very near to the 'Hilly Fields', a big open area that in 1857 was occupied by Lundhill Colliery and a brickworks. As children we used the area to play football, cricket and fantasy war games. There was no other open space available as play space for children from the slum areas, and while playing our games we had little knowledge at the time of the terrible disaster that had taken place beneath the ground on which we played.

In the 1850's, Lundhill was a small mining village nestled in a valley between the villages of Wombwell and Hemingfield, and was built to accommodate mine workers and their families. There wasn't much at Lundhill except the colliery, a brickworks, one long row of miners' cabins, a pub, a few small shops and a Wesleyan Chapel; just enough infrastructure to supply the basic needs of those supplying labour for the mine. All that exists of Lundhill today is the Lundhill Tavern that boasts one of the finest restaurants in the district. Strangely, this building started its days simply as a meeting place where mine owners would gather to decide the price of coal and the wages they would pay their miners, before eventually being used as a pub.

The hill above the valley was always referred to as the 'Hilly Fields' and later in the 1970's was used to build a small golf course named 'The Hillies'. For some strange reason Lundhill and the tragedy and loss of life that occurred there seemed wanted to be forgotten or ignored. Nowhere was there any indication that golfers should be aware that they played their sport on top of the grave of many men and boys. Only after I campaigned vigorously did the local council eventually erect a monument, but then got the number of men and boys still buried underground completely wrong on the inscription. Perhaps full disclosure might have discouraged golfers from using the course.

Life was grim for the Lundhillers who went to work at the mine only because it was a better alternative to starving or the dreaded workhouse. Wages were small and families large forcing some miners to send their young children down the mine in order to put food on the table. The hours were long and backbreaking for men and boys who were also in constant fear of explosions, rock falls and other accidents that claimed many lives. In an area of less than ten square miles in the Valley more than 750 men and boys were killed in pit explosions between 1850 and 1875. In all the newspaper reports of pit explosions, casualties were always listed as men and boys but it is an undeniable fact that details of women and girls killed in mining accidents were never reported and deliberately withheld from the British public who would have been horrified had such details been revealed.

The Lundhill pit disaster.... ....19th February 1857....

Lundhill colliery was owned by Messrs Simpson, Stewart, Taylor and Galand and at the time was the deepest mine in the Valley. The owners had sunk a shaft 215 yards deep to the 'Barnsley seam' and were fully aware of the nauseous nature of the seam as six men had been killed in an explosion when the shaft was being sunk.

Thursday the 19th February 1857 seemed just like any other day at the mine. A day shift of 220 men had started their twelve hour shift at 6am. At noon, 22 of the men who lived near the mine surfaced to take their mid-day meal while the others stayed underground. Shortly after noon a huge explosion shook the ground around Lundhill and flames shot up over 20 yards above the shaft headgear.

Fire engines raced to the colliery but there was little they could do. Viewers (managers) from nearby collieries arrived at the mine to offer their services. Three hours after the blast a team of experienced managers and miners volunteered to descend the shaft to assess the situation and to see if there was any chance of rescuing survivors. At the bottom of the shaft they found 20 badly burnt and injured men and were able to send them up to the surface. A little further on from the pit bottom dead men and pit ponies were tangled together in heaps. They then moved on 400 yards in all directions passing scores of corpses but found no further sign of life. Finding the smoke and afterdamp two strong they decided to return to the surface before they became cut-off.

Just after 7pm a sheet of flame rose more than 100 feet above the pit shaft lighting-up the sky for miles around and illuminating the grief stricken miners' families as they waited for news of their loved ones. After discussions between owners and managers it was concluded there was no hope of further rescue and the only hope of putting the fire out and save the mine for future use was to flood the mine with water from a nearby stream. After the mine had been flooded observations and temperature tests were taken at regular intervals to ensure all areas in the seam were cooling down.

Only on the 17th April and two months after the explosion was it considered safe to start a search to recover bodies. Teams of experienced miners were organised twelve to a team who worked for four hours with two experienced deputies and an assistant manager to supervise them. The work of recovering bodies was described as hazardous and odious and men tasked with handling the bodies found the stench unbearable. A medical adviser was in attendance and deodorising agents had to be used along with tar and chloride of lime. Advice was given by the Inspector of Burial Grounds but no record exists of the decision to close off the worst affected part of the seam.

By the 22nd May 100 bodies had been recovered and by the end of July all the bodies that could be found had been removed from the mine. A total of 190 men and boys died in the explosion. 149 were buried at the All Saints Churchyard, Darfield, while 41 men and boys remained buried underground at the colliery site and underneath the 'Hillies' golf course. After investigations with the late George Beedan, an authorative local historian on mining affairs in the Valley, we were able to establish that the missing bodies were concealed at the furthest point of the seam and probably where the explosion first took place and was considered by the rescuers to be too unsafe to enter. That part of the seam was later sealed off to prevent any further seepage of gas into the restored working areas in the seam.

Recovering bodies from the mine was a grim task for those involved. None of the victims had been positively identified as their bodies had been blown apart and were seriously decomposed after up to five months in the flooded mine. Some identification must have been possible by other means as there is a list of names of those who were buried in the Darfield Churchyard. Of the 149 interred in four mass graves, 110 are named and 39 were buried name unknown. As far as it can be ascertained 37 boys died in the explosion:-

Aged 10 years – 6
11 years – 2
13 years – 4
15 years – 3
16 years – 2
17 years - 20

The Kellet family lost seven members of their family. Some families suffered the loss of all their male relatives. The disaster left 92 widows and 220 fatherless children. Three years after the disaster 48 of the younger women had re-married. There only alternative would have been to take their children to the workhouse. A national relief fund raised £10 676 but the Lundhill Colliery Company contributed only £500. Little is known how the funds were finally distributed.

After the disaster....

At the inquest, the Coroner Mr Badger, found the disaster to have been caused by the explosion of carburetted hydrogen gas but there was no conclusive evidence to show the cause of ignition and he told the jury they should not come to a decision there was criminal negligence, even though throughout the inquiry evidence had been given of clear acts of negligence by colliery officials. Coroner Badger went on to say there was however laxity of discipline and non-observance of special rules but no blame should be attached to the proprietors of the colliery. He concluded by saying, "Every practicable effort should be set forth to raise miners to a higher moral and mental standard". It seems that the Coroner was laying the blame on the miners but what their moral and mental state had to do with the cause of the disaster is not clear. Having been absolved of responsibility for the disaster the owners were also absolved from paying compensation.

There are some confusing figures in the Coroner's report. It was reported there were 220 underground at the mine at the time of the explosion, but 22 had left the mine at lunchtime and 20 were rescued from the bottom of the shaft leaving a total of 178 underground and who were killed in the explosion. However the Coroner reported a death toll of 190 leaving 12 unaccounted for. It was widely believed that the 12 were probably women and girls and nobody was prepared to admit or to testify they were there. The figures also confirm that 41 bodies must have been left unrecovered underground in the sealed-off part of the seam. Although the Coroner confirmed 149 bodies were buried at the Darfield All Saints Churchyard the obelisk erected in memory of the mine victims states only 146. The reason for this could be that the mason did not have space for (nine) so reduced the number to (six) making it 146. Such was the ambivalence towards coal miners at the time that few people in authority would have noticed, cared or objected to the error.

The Barnsley Old Oaks.... ....colliery disaster....12th December 1866....

No lessons were learnt by the government and mine-owners regarding mine safety after the Lundhill pit disaster. Few new regulations were implemented to ensure the safety of miners working underground and the employment of young children continued as they were a source of cheap labour for unscrupulous mine-owners whose only concerns was their profit. It was only a matter of time before another major disaster struck the mining communities of the Valley.

The accident rate in the Valley continued to increase remorselessly. Miners had to face the prospect of crippling accidents and death on a daily basis and for those who survived, the only prospect in older age was a lingering death from lung disease and the pain of being unable to financially support their families after being tossed aside with no provision for their old age.

Inevitably, the failure by the government to legislate for mine safety eventually resulted in another and even worse pit disaster. On Wednesday the 12th December 1866, an underground explosion occurred at the Old Oaks colliery Barnsley killing 334 men and boys. The explosion was so fierce it was heard three miles away. The following day a team of volunteers went down the shaft to see if there was anything could be done. Tragically a second explosion occurred killing all 27 volunteer rescue workers. After a further fourteen explosions it was decided to seal the mine and abandon it for any further use.

A monument to the heroism and self-sacrifice of the 27 volunteer rescue workers was erected at the top of Kendray Hill overlooking the site of the tragedy that had appalling consequences for the surrounding mining communities that supplied the labour for the mine.

A national appeal to support families of the victims raised £48 000, an amount believed by some to be bigger than necessary. It was claimed that those responsible for disbursing the money to the families wanted to make sure the widows' station in life did not improve and were no better off than they would have been had their husbands not died. Such was the disrespect accorded to the coal mining communities at the time.

The miners' strike of 1893....

The working and living conditions of miners in the Valley and other mining areas did not improve. It would seem the British nation was oblivious to the inhuman way miners and their families were treated which resulted in many strikes and lock-outs. However, the miners were unable to win against the mine-owners who seized every small fluctuation in the price of coal to reduce their wages. In 1891 the market dropped heavily followed by severe cuts in wages by mine-owners.

After many struggles, miners in the Valley were eventually able to organise and formed the Yorkshire Miners' Association (YMA). Membership at first was small but as smaller groupings amalgamated membership grew to over 50 000 by 1889, giving the YMA a stronger negotiating position at local and national level. Later in the same year the Miners' Federation of Great Britain (MFGB) was formed giving the miners an even stronger voice in their dealings with mine-owners and the government.

By 1892 the falling price of coal created a surplus of coal stocks at most mines that allowed mine-owners to reduce wages even further. At the 1892 conference of the MFGB several initiatives were implemented such as a 'stop week' when miners would not work and was intended to reduce surplus stocks, but after just one month it was called off. An attempt was then made to limit production by only working five days a week and having a 'play Saturday' but this met with limited success as it was not fully supported. The simple fact was that miners' wages were already so small that they could not afford to lose a day's wages let alone a full weeks pay. Families were already close to starvation level.

On the 30th June 1893, mine-owners called the unions' representatives to a meeting in London and informed them that wages would have to be reduced by 18%. The YMA unanimously rejected the proposal as did all the other union branches throughout the MFGB. Consequently on the 28th July over 200 000 underground and surface workers went on strike and by the end of August the number had increased to over 300 000. In line with union policy no members were allowed to work except for attending to the needs of pit ponies and essential mine maintenance.

The strike was fully supported by all mining communities whose very existence was under threat, but there were incidents of violence against a few 'blacklegs' who wanted to continue working. After some mine-owners and their property were attacked by gangs of youths whose actions were strongly condemned by the union, police had to be called but as incidents of violence increased leaving the police unable to cope, the government authorised the use of troops to protect mine-owners and their properties. Fifty mounted Dragoons arrived in Barnsley on the 7thSeptember and two days later a company of soldiers from the Artillery barracks at Hillsborough marched into Orgreave Colliery. The soldiers were supplemented with additional police reinforcements drafted into the affected areas, clearly demonstrating the government was on the side of the mine-owners.

Due to divisions in the union the MFGB met and agreed to submit a ballot to all branches on three propositions. One was whether wages should be reduced by 18% as proposed by the mine-owners or any lesser percentage. Two, was whether the mine-owners offer of arbitration should be accepted, and three was whether all those who could do so should resume work at the old wages.

As the branches went through the voting process incidents of violence increased and particularly at Manvers Main Mexborough, Houghton Main, Darfield Main and Mitchell's Main. A meeting at Wombwell attended by over 2 000 miners resolved that all men had to be withdrawn out of the mines. A motion to march-on Hoyland Silkstone colliery to ensure work had ceased was defeated, but even so 700 men declared they would march regardless, resulting in further acts of violence at Hoyland and Rockingham.

Further serious acts of violence and damage to property occurred at the Featherstone Manor Colliery owned by a Mr Shaw and Ackton Hall colliery owned by Lord Masham. Disputes between the striking miners and mine-owners grew as the miners suspected coal was being secretly loaded. As the violence worsened the manager of Ackton Hall colliery went to Wakefield to seek assistance from the Chief Constable and found that Lord St.Oswald, owner of Nostell Colliery had also requested assistance.

Mine-owners believed the situation was so serious that military intervention was necessary. After a meeting of magistrates of the Staincross Division, 54 men of the 1st.Battalion South Staffordshire Regiment arrived at Wakefield railway station and were divided into two sections. One was sent to Nostell Colliery and the other consisting of 28 men under the command of a Captain Barker was sent to Ackton Hall, Featherstone. News spread quickly through Featherstone village of the soldiers' arrival and an angry mob demanded to Captain Barker that he and his men should leave. Fires were started in several places and property was damaged by the mob that had grown to over 2000. When stones were thrown at the soldiers Captain Barker formed his men into line about five yards in front of the mob and gave the order to fix-bayonets. The attending magistrate read the 'riot-act' and warned the mob that if they did not leave peacefully their presence would constitute a felony.

Several soldiers were injured by stone throwers and the driver of a nearby train was attacked and injured. The magistrate decided that the troops should open-fire but asked Captain Barker if blanks could be fired first. Barker replied that it would be against regulations and ordered two of his men to fire but at ground line. At first the mob was stunned into silence until a shouting striker claimed, 'they are only firing blanks'. This encouraged the mob to move forward causing Captain Barker to order a section of 8 men to open-fire. The crowd was stunned as two men dropped dead and a further two were seriously injured.

An official inquiry (the Bowen Commission) was appointed to establish the circumstances of the disturbances at Featherstone, but it concluded that although misjudgements had been made the authorities were absolved of any wrongdoing.

In the meantime balloting of the three proposals put forward by the MFGB was still taking place. When the result was announced the YMA miners had rejected all three proposals, but by mid-October over 37 000 Federation members had returned to work while 230 000 remained on strike. But life was getting increasingly tough for the miners and their families as the union had to keep reducing the already meagre strike pay which was all the miners had. As winter closed in, families and particularly children were in desperate circumstances. Charities set-up soup kitchens for the starving families, then the communities were ravaged with a big increase in diphtheria and tuberculosis; typhoid fever started to spread rapidly among bodies too weak to resist.

The government was faced with a deepening economic crisis and were alarmed that if the dispute continued that it would permanently damage the country's industrial export trade, so they called both sides to a conference chaired by Lord Roseberry. A settlement was eventually agreed that would enable the miners to return to work at the old rate of wages until the 1st February 1894 allowing time for a board of conciliation to be established with fourteen members from each side.

The talks dragged on with the miners claiming a mixed victory. They had held out against a reduction in wages and working conditions. In reality neither side won as the disputes continued from one year to the next. The major gain was that after the strike the YMA and the MFGB were in a much stronger position to confront the mine-owners and the government and most importantly had demonstrated to their members that with unity their union could fight and protect the interests and welfare of the miners.

Valley men and the Boer war....

As the population of the Valley slowly recovered from the trauma of the Lundhill and Old Oaks colliery disasters and continuous confrontations with mine-owners, history continued to march onwards. In 1856 the Crimean War had ended after the appalling incompetence of the British military establishment had cost the lives of thousands of men who died from sickness, neglect and criminal decision making on the field of battle.

Lord Chelmsford managed to further disgrace the British military in 1879 by carelessly separating the forces under his command in Zululand, South Africa. His action resulted in the massacre of 1700 British soldiers by warriors of the Zulu King Cetshwayo. Trying to retain some credibility for her incompetent military, Queen Victoria authorised the award of eleven Victoria Cross medals to the defenders of Rorke's Drift where a single company of British soldiers had held the might of Cetshwayo's Zulu warriors at bay. Although there were undoubted individual acts of heroism among the defenders, Victoria's over the top awards to save face for her military commanders went dangerously close to devaluing the award of the Victoria Cross.

The first documented record of the involvement of working-class men from the Valley in the historic battles fought by Britain appears to be in the Anglo-Boer war in 1899-1902. The Boers, Dutch speaking farmers had developed large tracts of agricultural land in South Africa and had become alarmed at the influx of English speaking people hoping to benefit from the discovery of goldfields in the Transvaal. Boers were by nature a fiercely independent people who were unjustifiably described by Queen Victoria as a 'horrid people' who needed to be taught a big lesson. Little was Her Majesty aware at the time just how big a lesson her own aristocrats and generals were about to learn from the 'horrid' Boer farmers.

Britain and the Boers were soon on the brink of war. On the 11th October 1899, Boer President Paul Kruger, demanded British troops withdraw from the borders of the Boer Republic. This didn't happen and the two sides were soon locked in battle and a war in which Rudyard Kipling said, 'Taught the British no-end of a lesson'.

It's an unfortunate fact of British military history that since the victories of the Duke of Marlborough, General Wolfe at Quebec, Nelson at Trafalgar and the Duke of Wellington at Waterloo, the British military commanded by aristocrats were mostly incompetent and devoid of military skills. After Wellington and up to and including WWI, they were responsible for the unnecessary deaths of thousands of British soldiers.

The Crimean War and the Charge of the Life Brigade on the 25th October 1854 was an unmitigated disaster. Although the charge was carried-out by extremely brave men, their commanders were found wanting. Due to the serious mismanagement of resources, equipment, food and medicine, over 5000 men died of cholera and malaria within the first few weeks of arriving in the Crimea. Of the 21 000 British soldiers who died in the Crimean disaster only 3000 were killed in action or died of wounds. All the others died of disease, neglect and the result of an incompetent military establishment.

Although the Crimean war was an unmitigated disaster, the military establishment learnt no lessons. Incredibly the same leadership of aristocrats and sons of the establishment educated at Eton, Harrow and such places were still in place to repeat the same mistakes in South Africa fighting the Boers. Mismanagement, incompetence mixed with incredible bravery resulted in heavy casualties before General Kitchener devised a plan to break the Boers by burning their farms, killing their cattle and sending their women and children into what were little more than concentration camps, where many of them died in appalling conditions; earning an hatred against the British that has never gone away and remains a stain on the British military establishment.

The involvement of Valley men in the Boer war is recorded on a memorial to the 43 men who died in the war and which is implanted into the side wall of the former Wombwell Town Hall on the Station Lane side of the building.

Apart from sons of aristocrats and wealthy landowners in the Valley, only a few working-class Valley men would have been recruited to join the army before WWI. While education standards were not a priority for service in the ranks, health requirements were rigorous as few medical services were available for the lower-ranks in the event of sickness. It was most unlikely that men from the mining areas would have been able to meet the health standards required.

The miners' struggle....the Liberal Party....................and the birth of the Labour Party....

It's difficult to put into writing and describe the extent of the struggle the mining communities in the Valley braved to establish a mere existence in a country where they were constantly treated as barbarous and sub-normal. But in spite of all the loathing and misconceptions by most British citizens living their lives in relative luxury compared to the miserable and degrading existence of mining families, they fought on and the more they fought the more they were made to suffer. However, their determination was relentless and their solidarity began to achieve the results they craved and were prepared to suffer for.

After years of struggle with mine-owners, the South Yorkshire Miners' Association (YMA) was formed in 1881 and later helped to establish the Miners' Federation of Great Britain (MFGB) in 1889. The YMA and MFGB used its new strength to strive for better pay and working conditions for its members while at the same time trying to work positively to achieve conciliation with mine-owners.

As the strength of the miners' federation grew they pushed for greater involvement in the community life of the Valley with members joining Trades Councils and actively participating in local politics. Miner's involvement in local communities and politics was given a huge boost when John Mansell was elected to the School Board of Barnsley Town Council, previously the exclusive reserve of the local big-wigs. Benjamin Pickard a miners' leader was elected to the West Riding County Council and later served as an Alderman before being elected an MP. William Parrott, a YMA agent was elected to Parliament after the death of Pickard and was appointed the first working-class Justice of the Peace in 1904. Eventually the political and community involvement of miners' leaders started to have an impact in the Valley communities where they were active; resulting in a strong unity that enabled the miners to become a force to be reckoned with.

The Liberal Party was the dominant political Party in the Valley constituencies and had held the Barnsley Division parliamentary seat since 1855, but a by-election was required after the resignation of Earl Compton, the sitting MP, on the death of his father and his own elevation to the peerage. The Liberal Party had always been strong supporters of the miners whose support at elections had helped them to win and hold seats. With the growing strength of the YMA the Liberal Party was prepared to accept a YMA nomination for the vacant Barnsley seat in order to strengthen their support from the miners. The YMA put forward Joseph Walton knowing he would be an effective voice in Parliament.

Although the outcome of the by-election was never in any serious doubt and the Liberal Party would hold the seat, the potential outcome was threatened when the Independent Labour Party put up a candidate in opposition. In the event Walton secured the seat with a big majority mostly secured with the massive support of the miners.

The YMA in the Valley continued to grow and the leadership became more effective in dealing with mine-owners, but this didn't stop the strikes, lock-outs and mass-evictions from company housing making many families homeless and forced out onto the streets. By 1904 a new leadership emerged after the deaths of several top leadership members of the YMA and the election to office of Herbert Smith as President, Mike Wandsworth as general-secretary and Joe Hall as agent.

The first rumbles of the Labour Party in the Valley started to be felt. Throughout the 1880's, Keir Hardie had been indefatigable in fighting for working-men candidates for parliamentary seats. At the 1887 TUC congress, Hardie, a new member representing Ayrshire miners supported a separate Party and break away from Liberal Party candidates. This resulted in the formation of the Independent Labour Party (ILP). On a visit to the Valley to boost ILP membership he was chased out of town by Wombwell miners. The support for the Liberal Party among miners was still very strong at that time.

When the general-election of 1906 loomed there were strong objections from the ILP against Liberal Party nominated candidates, but Wandsworth and Hall were duly nominated by the YMA for the two Liberal Party allocated seats of Hallamshire and Normanton. The ILP alleged that Valley miners lagged seriously behind those in Lancashire because of their attachment to officials for Liberalism. In spite of strong opposition from the ILP, Joseph Walton was once again elected to represent Barnsley as a Liberal Party MP and in 1922 he was created a Baronet.

A Labour Representation Committee (LRC) was set-up in 1900 by the TUC who at the time had a membership of 550 000. At the conference Keir Hardie successfully moved a motion proposing there should be a distinct Labour Party in Parliament based upon recognition of the class-war and that the Labour Group should be independent of all other political Parties including the Liberal Party. At the following 1905 conference, Hardie again urged delegates not to mix-up the Labour movement with the Liberal Party and that they should endeavour to remain independent.

Keir Hardie continued to fill confidence among Labour Party members and after the general-elections in 1910 he was elected leader of the Labour Party group in Parliament. But some of Hardie's policies were not popular with many of the Labour MP's and especially the 'gentlemen' MP's who much to his opposition had managed to gain membership in the Party. Hardie was outspoken on issues such as Women's Suffrage, self-rule for India and equal rights for non-whites in South Africa. He also tried to organise a strike against Britain's participation in WWI and was accused of being a traitor. Hardie died on the 25th September 1915. Most of what he fought for in Parliament was eventually achieved by a later and more enlightened Labour Party.

Unquestionably, Keir Hardie must be given credit for the formation and growth of the Labour Party, although what he would have thought about Tony Blair's 'New Labour' and the betrayal of cherished socialist policies that he and the founding fathers of the unions and the Labour Party had fought so hard for, is a matter for conjecture.

The Liberal Party in the Valley continued to hold the Barnsley seat until 1929 when John Potts took the seat for the Labour Party, but the seat was taken back by Lib/Lab candidates in 1931 and 1935 before Frank Collindridge won the seat for the Labour Party in 1938. Roy Mason then won the seat in 1950 and held it until his retirement gaining a reputation as one of the Party's most successful MP's. A close confidant of Prime Minister Harold Wilson, Mason served under him in several senior Cabinet posts before retirement and his elevation to the House of Lords.

From relative peace...... the Valley was dragged into war....

After the trauma of living through many years of near starvation and neglect and the emergence of a strong union and Labour Party, the Valley settled down to a relatively brief period of peace and progress. The involvement of working-men in community affairs had started to improve the miners' quality of life. However, they still had to battle for better wages and working conditions, but the Labour Party had started to be a powerful force giving hope for the future for the miners and their families.

Unfortunately, just as the world started to be at peace, monarchs and aristocrats in Europe and Russia started to fall out causing tremors that eventually caused an earthquake that shook the world rigid. Many believed the war that came so quickly would not last longer than a few months and the monarchs and aristocrats would be back in their palaces by Christmas. It was not to be. The men from the Valley marched to war in their thousands. Only a few returned.

War is declared....

The prelude to WWI and the involvement of Britain, the British Empire, Europe and the United States of America in one of the bloodiest wars in history started on the 14th June 1914 after the assassination of Archduke Franz Ferdinand, heir to the throne of the Austrian-Hungarian Empire in Sarajevo. Although it was widely believed it was the assassination of the Archduke that caused the war; in fact, Germany's Kaiser Wilhelm II had started planning for war as early as 1884 when he started to build-up Germany's navy which caused alarm in European nations. The Kaiser decided not to renew Germany's treaty with Russia and instead pursued a treaty with Austria. France and Russia fearing the German and Austrian alliance immediately signed a treaty creating two distinct blocks.

Britain considered the new political groupings to be a threat to Britain's security and decided to conclude agreements with France and Russia that effectively divided Europe into two armed camps making war to seem inevitable. The Kaiser had started his advanced preparations for war in 1912 with the intention of breaking French power and reducing France and Belgium to vassal status while carving out a colonial empire in Africa; creating a customs union that would make Germany an economic powerhouse.

Within one month of Archduke Ferdinand's assassination, Austria-Hungary had declared war on Russia who they held responsible for the assassination. The Russian army successfully repulsed the attacking Austria-Hungary invasion, but Germany in support of Austria-Hungary declared war on Russia on the 3rd August 1914. After Germany invaded Belgium on the 4th August 1914, Britain declared war on Germany and Austria-Hungary. The President of the United States, Woodrow Wilson, declared a policy of neutrality.

After the Anglo-Boer war which ended in 1902, the British War Minister, Richard Haldane had wisely created the British Expeditionary Force (BEF) in the event it became necessary to be involved overseas again. At the outbreak of war in 1914 the BEF consisted of seven infantry divisions based in France and Belgium. Originally consisting of 120 000 men the BEF was divided into the First and Second Army both under the command of Sir John French. A Third Army was added in July 1915 and a Fourth Army in March 1916.

On Tuesday the 4th August 1914, The Prime Minister Mr Herbert Asquith told the House of Commons that an ultimatum had been delivered to the German government that unless Germany withdrew its demand on Belgium to allow German troops to pass through Belgium territory, then the ultimatum would come into effect and a state of war would exist.

Residents in the Valley and the British nation waited in breathless anxiety as the hours ticked away. In London, cities, towns and the villages of the Valley, crowds of people gathered together waiting to see if peace was at an end; unknowingly witnessing the beginning of the slaughter of British and European manhood on a scale never imagined. When the ultimatum expired, the Prime Minister told the House of Commons that Britain had entered the fray and had a duty to go to Belgium's assistance and was bound by honour to support France.

The Valley went to war....

Lord Kitchener had already been recalled to London to organise the British armies and was appointed Secretary of State for War. His famous recruiting poster and his pointing finger shouting out, 'Your Country Needs You', was instrumental in the recruitment of over 1 200 000 recruits by the end of 1914.

The first battle in which the BEF was involved was at 'Mons' where the BEF caught between two German armies was almost cut-off. The first major battle in which General Sir Douglas Haig was in command was at Neuve-Chapelle and resulted in an advance of 1000 yards at a cost of 12 000 casualties, a strong indication of what was still to come. Haig's next big battle was at Loos where confusion between Haig and Sir John French the Commander in Chief, resulted in 8000 casualties in the first hour. Casualties would have been higher but for the fact as recorded in the history of the 15th German Reserve Division, that the German soldiers were so nauseated by the sight of the massacre on the Leichenfield (field of corpses) that when the British soldiers started to retire, no shots were fired at them for the rest of the day. The tragedy of the two battles was a serious indictment on the foolish and costly strategy that was used by British commanders throughout the war; at enormous cost in British lives.

Haig used the blunders at Loos to oust Sir John French and was himself appointed Commander-in-Chief three months later; achieved mostly through his connections with the Royal Family. Before the war, Haig realised that if he was going to progress to top senior ranks he would need to be married and more importantly to someone close to the Royal Family. In 1905 he met and made a proposal of marriage all within 72hours. His career promised further advancement when the woman whom he married was a personal attendant and favourite of the Queen. Haig was also the first man outside the royal circle to be married in the Buckingham Palace private chapel.

Already the tragedy of the Somme was beckoning. Before the war Britain had a system of voluntary service for the regular army. This was backed-up with national reserves who were former trained ex-soldiers who had volunteered to serve time on the reserve lists and in the Territorial Army. Reservists in the Valley volunteered in their thousands to rejoin their regiments. Some of the men selected from the Valley formed part of a unit accepted for the 5th Battalion the York and Lancaster Regiment (The Terriers) who were wildly cheered by the townspeople of Barnsley as they bade farewell at an emotional parade outside Barnsley Town Hall, attended by local dignitaries from across the Valley. Ever so smartly, 'The Terriers' marched off to war.

Lord Kitchener realised that as losses in Flanders escalated that the small regular army and reservists of the BEF could not last long, and that even with a second wave of reservists and Territorial's, they would not be able to cope with the terrible attrition taking place. Kitchener realised the army was going to need at least 500 000 men very quickly and made his 'Britain Needs You Appeal'. Nowhere was the response more greater than in the Valley.

The battle for Serre, the Somme, 1st July 1916...............'THE PALS' 13th & 14th Battalions............the York and Lancaster Regiment....

The Valley had already sent two territorial companies of the 5th Battalion the Yorks and Lancs, 'The Terriers', to boost the strength of the BEF in France, but there was concern among the male population in the Valley that they were not being allowed to play their part in fighting the enemy. After Lord Kitchener launched his appeal for 500 000 men local dignitaries from across the Valley decided to take a hand in recruiting for Lord Kitchener's new army. Most of the volunteers from the Valley were miners who had never left their home territory. Their patriotic zeal was strengthened at the prospect of getting away from the pit and going overseas, and as everybody was saying, 'the war would be over by Christmas'.

The concept of PALS battalions was already being pioneered and this motivated Valley civic leaders to send a telegram to Lord Kitchener offering to raise a battalion of 1100 men to be recruited from the Valley district. Kitchener quickly responded and accepted the offer. Formation of PALS battalions particularly appealed to local men as it meant they would be serving with their mates and neighbours from their home towns and villages who also spoke the same language. The prospect of serving with regiments full of foreigners did not appeal to them. Civic leaders pressed the appeal for volunteers with great enthusiasm and even encouraged wives and sweethearts to get their men to enlist. Posters were erected advising 'Women of Britain' say 'GO', with a picture of mothers with young children watching their men marching off to war. Captain H.P. Smith Commander of a Territorial detachment speaking at a presentation ceremony asked young women to use their influence to get their sweethearts to volunteer. Just how many of those young women would regret the influence they exerted on their men can only be speculated.

The recruitment campaign was intensified and eventually recruitment of local men from the Valley reached the target of 1100 needed to form a battalion, but the number of men wanting to enlist continued to increase to the extent that it was decided to request permission to form a second battalion. Authority for this was soon given and the Valley authorities were informed by the War Office that the two battalions would be the 13th and 14th Battalions of the York and Lancaster Regiment. The 13th was formed with 500 men and the 14th with 1100 men.

Although the response to volunteer had far exceeded expectations, it would seem nobody in authority had considered the question of command and leadership of the new recruits. All the regular and territorial officers had already been called to the colours and involved in the fierce battles taking place and where many of them had become casualties. There being no other option the War Office gave the Mayor of Barnsley and other Valley officials and dignitaries authority to appoint officers and senior non-commissioned officers who were then to put together a training programme.

There was already a disaster in the making. The men appointed officers were mostly local business men, town councillors and young men from prominent families such as Tom Guest, Councillor Charles Plumpton and Jack Brass the manager of Houghton Main Colliery. With the exception of Colonel Joseph Hewitt (temporary commander of the 13th) and Captain Tom Guest, most of the officers had no military experience or training.

Training for the 13th and 14th was way below the requirement for troops being sent into action. Training that did take place was mostly basic parade ground drill, target shooting and charging with fixed-bayonets, the minimum required when military commanders required 'cannon fodder' to plug the gaps for which they were reluctant to waste fully trained and well equipped regiments.

Colonel Hewitt was however replaced and command of the 13th was given to the younger Lt.Colonel Edmund Wilford, ex Indian Army, who had already had battle experience in France and who took over command six weeks before the battalion departed for Egypt. When the troopship 'Andania' docked at Malta to take on coal, officers and sergeants were allowed shore leave but the other ranks were confined to the ship. Thirteen days after leaving England the ship docked at Port Said, Egypt.

After almost two years in Egypt the men from the Valley, mostly miners, were used almost entirely on labouring duties resulting in the men feeling their patriotism and will to fight was being abused by the authorities. However, as the losses in France escalated at a rapid rate, the battalion was put on alert with the men excited that they were going to France at last. After a thoroughly unpleasant journey by sea they eventually landed at the Port of Marseilles on the 16th March 1916. The countdown to disaster at Serre had begun.

General Joffe's French army was taking a severe beating at Verdun and had already suffered 400 000 casualties; but were denying the German army a direct route to Paris. Joffe requested General Haig to launch an attack to take some pressure off the French and although Haig was keen, his commanders requested more time to prepare their troops and complete their training. Thwarted, Joffe went directly to the British High Command who authorised Haig to launch his already planned attack early. Training came to a stop and Haig marshalled his troops for the Somme offensive that would be recorded as one of the bloodiest battles in British military history.

Prior to the attack, Haig launched a seven day artillery bombardment against the German positions defending Serre and along the line of the Somme that was intended to cut the wire in front of the German positions and neutralise the enemy defences. However, it only succeeded in turning the ground British infantry would have to cross into a quagmire. The wire remained unbroken.

The Germans had built a series of trenches behind their front line trenches to which they could fall back, so that when the British bombardment rained down on the front line trenches, they simply moved back into the well prepared reserve trenches taking their guns and equipment with them. When the British bombardment ended they quickly moved back to the front line trenches with their guns and equipment intact; ready to meet the British infantry. British intelligence failed to identify the German tactics and continued to ignore front line patrol reports that the wire was not cut; demonstrating the lamentable staff failure at General Haig's headquarters.

Prior to the 13th and 14th moving into the front line for the attack on Serre, 10 officers and 174 men were selected to remain behind. These men were to be the nucleus of a new battalion should there be a disaster. This very action implied that General Haig new his tactics would involve serious losses and that the 'Pals' battalions were going to be sacrificed.

Every night before the attack patrols were sent out to check the effect of the artillery bombardment on the German defences. All the patrols reported that the wire had not been cut and the defences were still intact. It was known by experienced troops that an artillery barrage did not cut barbed-wire; it simply blew it up in the air and then it would settle back down on the ground, uncut. Some patrols reported that the Germans had increased the depth of the wire in some places.

Due to heavy rain the attack was postponed for 48 hours and 'Z' day rescheduled for the 1st.July with the attack to commence at 7.30am. This added another two days of misery for the waiting troops as their trenches filled with water and 'no-man's' land' turned into a quagmire that they were going to have to cross.

It was reported that the Corps Commander, General Hunter-Wilson, said before the attack, "He was extremely optimistic the wire had been blown away; there were no Germans left in the trenches and the British troops would be able to walk into Serre". This was said in spite of consistent reports from many patrols that the wire remained uncut all along the front line.

At his luxurious headquarters at the Chateau de Valvion in Beauquesne, General Haig was fast asleep as the Valley men of the 13th and 14th made their way up the front line to their position for the attack on Serre the next morning. Before falling asleep General Haig had wrote in his diary, 'The wire had never been cut so well and I have talked personally to all the Corps Commanders and all are full of confidence. The only doubt I have is regarding the 8thCorp (which included the 13th and 14th) which has no experience of fighting in France and has not carried out one successful raid. **Haig used this as one of his excuses for the disaster, but an enlightened investigator would have wanted to know why he placed inexperienced and untrained troops in the front line of the attack when he had other options. The answer was that he was fully aware the first waves were going to be cannon fodder for the enemy.**

After the war, Sir Douglas Haig wrote in his book 'Dispatches', the enemy position to be attacked was a very formidable character situated on a high and undulating tract of ground. The first and second systems each consisted of several lines of deep trenches well provided with bomb-proof shelters and with numerous communicating trenches connecting them. The front of the trenches in each system was protected by wire entanglements, many of them in two belts forty yards broad, built of iron stakes interlaid with barbed wire as thick as a man's finger. Defences of this nature could only be attacked after careful artillery preparation. Haig was able to write this after the war but failed to acknowledge that he knew nothing whatsoever about the state of the German defences when he launched the attack virtually blind, sacrificing unnecessarily the lives of thousands of British soldiers.

After the biggest artillery bombardment of the war General Haig still claimed the bombardment was a big success, although never acknowledging the German wire had not been cut and the German defences were still intact when he ordered the attack in complete ignorance of the real situation on the battlefield. As military strategists, Haig, his corps commanders and the general staff were totally incompetent and it was lamentable that neither the Chief of the General Staff, the Prime Minister nor King George took any action to replace him. The King was instrumental in Haig being appointed Commander-in-Chief of the BEF and was also responsible for allowing Haig's catastrophic leadership to continue.

One of the major reasons for many of the serious losses during the battles on the Somme was the failure of artillery support which Haig failed to identify. It was well known in military circles that being a cavalry man Haig knew very little about artillery and neither was it considered an important subject at Staff College. British artillery was notoriously inaccurate and consequently shells could not be used with reasonable safety less than 300 yards from advancing troops. In comparison the French artillery was able to fire a creeping barrage to within 60 yards of their troops as they advanced towards the enemy positions, reducing the first wave of casualties considerably. As the British infantry advanced the creeping barrage had to stop 300 yards from the enemy lines, exposing the troops to enemy gunners a long distance from the wire enabling the German gunners' time to zero in on the advancing troops. French infantry were often able to break through into the enemy trenches whereas British infantry seldom breached the wire.

The attack....

7.30am the 1st July 1916, the officers blew their whistles and the gallant men of the 13th and 14th Battalions the York and Lancaster Regiment the 'PALS' climbed up the step ladders and went over the top. One officer took a bullet in the head as he reached the top of the trench steps and fell back dead. His men didn't falter and went bravely forward; walking not charging as they had been ordered to save their strength for walking past the enemy lines and then the march into Serre. This was a serious fatal tactic dreamed-up by

General Haig's staff, for as the men were within 300 yards of the enemy positions the creeping artillery barrage stopped. Had they charged the positions instead of walking as instructed they could have covered the distance quickly, giving the enemy gunners less time to zero in on the advancing infantry.

When the British bombardment stopped, the German gunners moved swiftly from their rear positions where the British artillery had not reached them. With the British infantry still 300 yards away they had time to re-position their machine-guns and howitzers. The 13th and 14th continued to walk slowly forward with bayonets fixed and walked straight into an impenetrable wall of machine-gun fire. Men were falling all around but the survivors pressed forward. The PALS of the Sheffield battalion were the first wave to reach the wire but were virtually wiped-out within the space of a few minutes. The 13th and 14th followed the Sheffield men pushing towards the wire and taking heavy casualties. As one British wave was cut down another followed and another and then another and still the men pushed forward stumbling over the bodies of their dead comrades. A few even managed to reach the wire but there was no way through. The wire had not been cut, the enemy defences were still intact and the German gunners cut them down mercilessly in a cauldron of steel and blood. All along the front line of Serre and the Somme the same tragic failure was being reported. The Germans could not understand why British soldiers were sacrificing their lives marching slowly but heroically into their blazing guns and dying in thousands.

News that a disaster was taking place began to drift back to the rear lines but Major General O'Gowan still pressed Brigadier General Rees to send what troops he had left into the attack. To his credit, General Rees refused to commit more men until he had more definite news from the front. Although orders to renew the attack were sent from Corps HQ; these were rescinded as news of the disaster was passed back from Divisional HQ to Corps HQ.

A statement on the Somme offensive issued by the British Army High Command based in Paris on the 3rd July (two days after the disaster) read: "The first day of the Somme offensive is very satisfactory. The success is not a thunderbolt as has happened in previous operations, but it is important above all because it is rich in promise. It is no longer a question here of attempts to spear as with a knife. It is a rather slow, continuous and methodical push, sparing in lives, until the day when the enemy's resistance, incessantly hammered will crumple-up at some point. From today the first results of the new tactics permit one to await developments with confidence". Considering this statement it is not surprising that one observer remarked. **The British Army on the Somme were lions led by donkeys.**

By the end of the first day the Division suffered over 4500 casualties in front of Serre. Along the line of the Somme the British Army suffered over 60 000 casualties on the first day. Over 73 000 were missing presumed dead and had no known grave and are commemorated on the Thiepval war memorial in France. "Two years in the making - ten minutes in the destroying. That was our history"........John Harris.

Four weeks after the start of the Somme offensive, General Gough Commander of Haig's 5th Army issued a Routine Order that all burials were to be in trenches rather than individual graves. The first layer of corpses was to be buried four feet down with quick lime separating it from the next layer. Gough's order was an acknowledgement that his men were being killed faster than the grave diggers could dig graves.

The Somme offensive was planned by Haig to last fourteen days but only four months later did he finally concede he could make no advance and terminated the attack. The British and German armies had fired over 30 million shells at each other and suffered over one million combined casualties between them. British casualties were 600 000 in an area just seven square miles.

After the attack....

From reports made by Haig and others in the British High Command it became clear they had no confidence in the PALS (Kitchener's men) in their first major battle at Serre. The first day of the Somme was a black day in the reputation of the British military and Haig and his colleagues tried all they could to distance themselves from the disaster. Over 100 000 men went over-the-top on that fateful day and 60 000 became casualties within hours, but King George V lavished honours on the men responsible. Although Haig had said that he never trusted the PALS it did not stop him from using poorly prepared troops to carry out his ill-conceived plans regardless of how many lives would be lost.

The PALS could not be blamed for the disaster and it was morally indefensible for General Haig to have tried to do so. They did everything asked of them and laid down their lives for King and country. Not one man turned back as they marched slowly into the inferno of howitzer shells and machine-gun fire, while watching their comrades falling down all around them. Their courage and valour should never have been questioned. The question that should have been asked was that of the competence of the general staff and uncaring staff-officers living in luxury and safety well behind the enemy lines making blunder after blunder costing thousands of lives.

As news of the losses reached England and relatives were informed of those killed in action, the Valley was thrown into deep mourning. The PALS battalions of were such close units that in some streets all the young men had been killed and some families suffered the loss of two and sometimes three members of their family. The grieving was immense and as the deep mourning continued war memorials were erected in nearly every town and village in the Valley in memory of the fallen; a grim reminder for future generations of the sacrifice of Valley men at the altar of British military incompetence.

There were many mistakes before the men of the 13th and 14th went over-the-top at Serre. It needs to be said even if it is an unpalatable fact that the Mayor, councillors, dignitaries and the business community of the Valley, who motivated the men to volunteer for the PALS en-masse, share a large part of the blame for believing that all the men needed to win the war was patriotism and enthusiasm. They told the men they would be back home for Christmas. Many parents, wives and children had to spend Christmas grieving while their loved ones lay rotting in mass-graves in a foreign land.

The chief culprit of the Serre disaster was unquestionably General Sir Douglas Haig, who had continued to insist that the wire in front of the German defences had been cut when all patrol reports were telling him and his general-staff it was not. A cavalry man himself, he was obsessed with his plan for the infantry to break through the German defences and open a path for his cavalry regiments to charge triumphantly into Serre. It never happened and in an act of spiteful revenge he ensured few medals were awarded for what was one of the most epic battles of the Somme campaign. Eleven Victoria Cross medals were awarded at the battle against Zulus at Rorke's Drift, Natal, South Africa; the highest ever awarded in a single battle, but the British soldiers were defending a well fortified position against Zulus armed only with spears. In comparison only nine VC's were awarded to the army fighting on the first day along the entire line of the Somme and not one single VC was awarded to any of the PALS battalions in the attack although there were enough single acts of heroism to fill a history book. In a shameful act of spite Haig ensured the PALS did not receive the honours they undoubtedly deserved. His claim that the PALS were the weakest link in the line at Serre needs to be compared with his own personal conduct and that of his senior commanders.

The only senior officer to come out of the Serre debacle with any credit was Brigadier-General Rees, who had the courage to stop the slaughter and refused to send more men to a certain and unnecessary death. Although no action was taken against him he was relieved of his command two days later and ordered to return to England.

Haig used over one million men against the German positions on the Somme and although repeatedly suffering heavy casualties, he continued to throw his men against the German wire and massed machine-guns without any change in tactics or strategy. As winter approached he was forced to bring the Somme offensive to a close and by which time the BEF had suffered over 600 000 casualties under his command. Although severely criticised by Prime Minister Lloyd George who tried to remove him as Commander-in-Chief, Haig continued to command the BEF until the end of the war (mostly through the support he received from the King) by which time Britain and the nations of the Empire had suffered over three million casualties. For his dedicated leadership throughout the war and his service to Britain, King George V rewarded Haig by creating him the 1st Earl Haig. An act that was a stain on the memory of all those heroic men who Haig sent needlessly to their death and an insult to the many families left grieving for their men.

Financially the cost of the war was crippling to both sides. The cost to Germany was over $60 billion and to Britain and allies over $125 billion. These figures related to present day dollar values would show the cost to have been horrendous.

The real tragedy was that as the First World War came to an end, the seeds were already being sown for another World War.

After the war...........almost revolution....

After the trauma of war the Valley settled down to peace as families tried to cope with their losses. As seems to be the case in all wars, women always suffer the most and so it was in the Valley where many widows coping with large families had also to find work to feed their children while many old people were left without the support of their adult children. As the Valley tried to overcome yet another tragedy in their lives, the old battle for a living wage with the mine-owners resumed adding further misery to an already miserable existence.

When over 100 000 strikers raised the 'red flag' over George Square, Glasgow on the 31st January 1919, Britain trembled. The Bolshevik uprising in Russia had destroyed the Russian aristocracy and created a new order. China followed the same path and the Irish revolted against British rule.

The strikes in 1919 were the most serious ever seen in Britain and at a cost of 35 million working days lost, crippling the already fragile economy after the huge cost of the war. Among those joining the strike for the first time ever were members of the police and armed forces. Miners, transport workers and printers joined the strikers who had protested against the war throughout the war. The success of the Bolsheviks in creating a Soviet Russia motivated the strikers against greedy employers and an uncaring government. When the strikers demonstrated in Glasgow City Square, the Provost invited the strike leaders into the City Chambers for negotiations but as soon as the leaders were inside police charged the strikers with batons drawn. However the police came off worst and were driven from the square by the strikers.

The Cabinet were advised that the riot in Glasgow was not a strike but a Bolshevik uprising. Subsequently orders were issued to read the 'riot-act' authorising the use of troops issued with live ammunition. Orders were given not to use Scottish troops as it was feared they would join the strikers. A force of 12 000 troops with tanks and artillery from southern regiments were rushed to the area and the city encircled with barbed-wire and checkpoints. Most of the strike leaders were arrested, convicted and jailed. Willie Gallagher one of the key leaders said after the strike, "We were leading a strike when we should have been leading a revolution".

It is still debated as to what should have happened with many believing a revolution at that time would have been successful. In hindsight it would appear to have been extremely doubtful. The British government could not be compared with an abysmal Russian aristocracy or the disciplined British military with a Russian peasant army. A revolution would have met with a brutal iron fist that even the might of Germany could not overcome. And as one looks at Britain today, a revolution wasn't necessary.

From one war to the next.....the years of depression 1918 to 1939....

At the end of the war, Prime Minister Lloyd-George on the re-election of his government promised to build **'a land fit for heroes to live in'.** For a few years it looked as though the economy was improving enabling the working-class and surviving heroes the chance to enjoy a better life. But it didn't last; by 1921 industrial profits started to fall causing reductions in wages. As the economy continued to worsen, demobilised soldiers were unable to find work. By the summer of 1921 over 2 million were unemployed and as widespread suffering gripped the working-class, workers resorted to strikes.

At the 1923 general-elections the Labour Party won 191 seats and Ramsay MacDonald the Labour Party leader agreed to head a minority Labour government and became the first Labour Party Prime Minister. MacDonald was a doubtful socialist who it was said was influenced by his wealthy wife. However he was soon out of office after his government was defeated in a vote of confidence. In opposition he was again elected leader of the Labour group where he tried to present the Party as a moderate force in politics but caused great resentment when he refused to support the 1926 strike.

In 1925, mine-owners decided they had to reduce miners' wages after a drop in the price of coal, causing the TUC to respond by promising to support the miners in the dispute. A Royal Commission set-up by the government recommended the coal industry needed to be re-organised but rejected nationalisation and further recommended that a subsidy paid to miners be withdrawn and the miners' wages reduced. At the same time mine-owners decided on new terms of employment that included an extension of the seven-hour working day and a reduction in wages of 25%. They also announced that if the miners did not accept the new terms then they would be locked-out of their pits from the 1st May. This was devastating news for the miners in the Valley as the new terms meant they would be unable to buy food and basic essentials for their families, making a long and bitter strike their only option.

The TUC called an urgent meeting and after a long discussion decided they had no alternative but to call a 'general-strike' to protect miners' wages and working hours. Although the strike was due to start on the 3rd May, the Trades Councils and the Labour Party were not happy with the decision to strike and made frantic efforts to negotiate an agreement with the government and mine-owners. Prime Minister Stanley Baldwin agreed to negotiations with the TUC and for a while it seemed an agreement was going to be reached but after Baldwin was told that printers at the Daily Mail had refused to print an article critical of the strike, he broke off the negotiations.

When the strike began the TUC brought out workers in support from all the key industries including iron and steel workers, dockworkers, railway men, builders and printers. Over three million men went on strike and were later joined by engineers and shipyard workers.

On the 7th May, Sir Herbert Samuel chairman of the Royal Commission on the Coal Industry approached the TUC and offered to negotiate to end the strike and to which the TUC agreed without informing the miners' union of their intentions. A set of proposals were put to the TUC but Sir Samuel warned that any subsequent negotiations would require a reduction in wages. The TUC accepted the terms which were vigorously rejected on the issue of wages reduction when put to the Miners' Federation who felt badly betrayed by the TUC. Prime Minister Baldwin invited the TUC to Downing Street and the government was informed the 'general-strike' was off but they required a guarantee there would be no victimisation of miners' strike leaders. Baldwin refused and Lord Birkenhead a Cabinet minister present at the meeting wrote later; "The TUC's surrender was so humiliating that some instinctive breeding made one unwilling to look at them".

On the 21st June 1926 and eight weeks after the strike started, the government passed a Bill in the House of Commons that suspended the miners' 'seven working hours act' for five years, permitting a return to an eight hour working day. MP's voting on the Bill had no idea what it was like to work underground in horrific conditions with the constant threat of explosions and rock falls. Mine-owners then announced new terms of employment based on an eight hour working day. Furious miners refused to accept and decided to continue the strike believing the TUC had betrayed them.

Several months passed with hardships for the miners and their families in the Valley worsening day by day. Children on the verge of starvation were kept alive only by charities providing soup kitchens. Women combed muck stacks (spoil heaps) in search of pieces of coal to try and keep their children warm at night, but disease and child deaths increased rapidly. With no money for funerals children and babies were buried secretly and without a Christian burial around the perimeters of churchyards. Eventually it became too much for the miners having to watch their children slowly dying and in desperation some of them drifted back to work. By November the strike was over as most of the men had returned to work. After all the suffering and grief the miners were forced to accept lower wages and longer working hours. Many of the miners, particularly the strike leaders were victimised by the mine-owners who refused to employ them leaving them completely destitute as there was no other employment available in the mining villages.

In relation to the miners' struggle, Ramsay MacDonald's position as Labour Party leader needs to be considered; he refused to support the miners and the 1926 strike and endeavoured to present the Labour Party as a moderate force in British politics arguing that strikes should not be used as a political weapon and that the best way to obtain social reform was through parliamentary elections. It was believed his views were popular with the electorate and helped the Labour Party to return to government in the 1929 general-election.

However, Valley men were never going to forget MacDonald's betrayal and believed he was not a socialist but just another one of the elite who believed they were born to govern Britain. The Valley men were eventually proved right as MacDonald betrayed everything the Labour Party stood for in order to stay in high office with either the Tories or the Liberals.

Life in the Valley......between the wars....

It would seem that nearly all the local history of the Valley has been connected to the many wars and fierce battles in which many Valley men lost their lives fighting for their country and world peace. A look at the chronology of wars since the Duke of Wellington's victory at the battle of Waterloo in 1815, gives an indication of how the British nation has been continually caught-up in war.

The Crimean War 1853-1856

The Zulu wars in South Africa started around 1879 and lasted until 1887.
The Anglo-Boer War in South Africa 1899-1902

World War One 1914-1919

World War Two 1939-1945

The Korean War 1950-1953

Many years of sectarian terrorism in Northern Ireland

Suez 1957

The Falklands 1982 (recaptured within 74 days).

Iraq plus other areas of conflict such as Afghanistan and Kosovo

Libya in 2011.

Peace between the wars has only been periodic, but there was a life between the wars and the miners and their families in the Valley found their own way to enjoy their leisure time. After WWI some popular sports were the game of 'nipsy', whippet racing (a greyhound type dog) and pigeon racing along with many pub games and sing-along evenings in the local pub.

'Nipsy', is an old Valley game and played mostly by working-men and probably started prior to 1850 as a single player sport. Later, and probably around 1940 it became a team game and leagues were established, some of which were still in existence in 1990. The stick used for playing is shaped almost like a golf club (but smaller) which caused the game to be referred to as 'miners'golf'. The nipsy is a small round piece of wood which has to be placed on the top of an up-turned brick. Considerable skill and practice is required to hit the nipsy to make it rise (chipping) and as it rises striking the nipsy with the stick and driving it as far as possible,

Whippet racing was a very popular sport among the miners in the Valley. The sport is believed to have developed locally when peasants from agricultural areas moved into the mining areas seeking work and taking their 'snap' dogs with them. The peasants had used the dogs for entertainment by counting how many rabbits a dog could snap-up before they left a drawn circle. With the absence of many rabbits in their new surroundings they found their dogs would chase a waving rag just as eagerly. Rag racing became a popular pastime for miners and the whippet became known as the working-man's racehorse.

Pigeon racing has a cloth-cap image of the working man tending his pigeons in a shed at the bottom of his garden, but it is a world-wide sport. Her Majesty the Queen is a patron of the Royal Racing Club of Great Britain. Pigeons were always a big conversation in the tap-rooms of local pubs in the Valley.

It's probably true to say that through all the struggles, the wars and the battle to survive, the people of the Valley still found time for leisure, to laugh, to have fun and get on with their lives, even when the next struggle was just around the corner.

As life in the Valley seemed out of touch with many of the important events taking place at national and world level; the working and living conditions for miners and their families continued to be their biggest priority. Pit explosions continued and many miners still died in pit disasters and from industrial disease. But as the miners and their families suffered in silence, national events were taking place that soon plunged out of control and embroiled the world in another conflict that would result in the deaths of millions of soldiers and civilians on an epic scale.

World War Two....

Once again, the Valley, in spite of all its suffering at the hands of its governments, responded patriotically to the call for service. Able bodied men and women responded in their thousands to join the armed-forces, while those who were exempt such as miners and those in essential employments joined the Home Guard, ARP and many other civilian services.

The war lasted seven long years and as the casualty figures grew almost every street in the Valley saw the loss of loved ones killed in action, wounded or taken a prisoner of war. But in spite of all the losses and hardships that saw the nation teetering on starvation, the spirit of the British nation and its allies finally prevailed and Hitler and his Nazi criminals was finally defeated.

There were joyous scenes in the Valley when King George the VI announced VE Day-Victory over Europe. The Valley celebrated with street parties and bonfires and joyously welcomed home the returning of prisoners of war. But once again the grim task of placing the names of all those killed in action on the local war memorials had to begin and was another reminder of the terrible cost of war.

The cost of war....

The total human cost of the war for all the nations involved was over 34 million military personnel killed, wounded or missing in action and 24 million civilians killed or missing. It is difficult to understand how such a mass slaughter could have taken place and must surely never be allowed to happen again. But could it?

The cost although terrible was not only in the loss of lives, disabled people and millions displaced around the world, but also the economic cost. After the war Britain was almost financially bankrupt causing a great deal of industrial and political unrest and even more suffering for the working-class.

The Home Guard....

It was great fun watching 'Dad's Army' on television but while it was funny to watch it did not portray the reality of how important the Home Guard was in providing a second-line of defence for Britain if Hitler's threat of invasion had taken place. When the government made an appeal for men of all ages to volunteer, over 250 000 flooded police-stations to offer their services. Most of the men in the Valley who had wanted to enlist in the services had been prevented from doing so due to their employment being classified for essential war effort. The Home Guard gave them the opportunity to be able to serve their country in uniform and they signed-on in their thousands. When the Home Guard was finally stood down towards the end of the war in 1944 it consisted of over 1 793 000 volunteers.

Growing-up during World War II....

I was born in December 1935. Four years later Prime Minister Neville Chamberlain announced to the nation that Britain was at war with Germany. Six years later I was a schoolboy at Wombwell Secondary Modern School and I clearly remember one day running home from school at lunchtime (as part of my training for cross-country racing) across the feast field (the local fairground) when one of my mates came running towards me shouting, 'It's over, the war it's over'. I ran home even faster than usual and switched on the radio and listened to the news with my Mum. The war in Europe was over; Hitler had finally been defeated.

The war has been and is still a definitive period in my life. As children we were exposed to the fear of what Hitler would do to us if he won the war. We experienced the air-raid sirens and the fumble with gas-masks and stressed when military events went against our armed-forces. We worried when London and even cities close to us like Sheffield were bombed and ships bringing vital supplies across the Atlantic were sunk in large numbers and thousands of sailors were killed at sea. We witnessed the grief of those who lost loved ones' fighting heroically in the sky to keep the enemy at bay and also the fear felt by those whose men folk had been captured by the enemy and taken into German and Japanese prisoner-of-war camps.

My family was fortunate to own a radio and we would sit around anxiously waiting for news from the regular news broadcasts. Our daily newspaper the 'Daily Herald' was another supplier of news and when my Dad came home from nightshift, I would collect the newspaper from the front door and as he ate his breakfast I would sit on his knee and together we would read and discuss the progress of the war.

The first sign the war was a reality in the Valley came when air-raid shelters were built in backyards, school playgrounds and any place a big shelter could be built. Some shelters were brick and concrete built while smaller Anderson shelters were made of corrugated iron. Most schools had shelters built within close proximity.

When the air-raid sirens did sound, mostly at night and usually when Sheffield was being bombed; caring neighbours would rush to our house to help Mum get all the kids into the shelter, especially when dad was on night shift. One neighbour, Mrs Thorpe would always come for me and would nurse me on her knee throughout the raid. I still remember one night when we could hear the loud explosions of bombs and sitting with Mrs Thorpe near the door, I could see the sky all lit-up followed by big bangs which shook the shelter. Mrs Thorpe was saying to Mum, "Sheffielder's are getting it bad tonight".

One of the biggest fears was that the Germans would drop gas on the civilian population and the government had to dig deep to provide everybody with a gas-mask, including a special mask for babies that looked like a covered-over babies cot. Wearing the masks for the first time was claustrophobic but we soon adapted to them. What frightened us most was when periodically a gas test van would come to school. We had to put our gas-masks on and sit inside the van and were told that if our eyes started to smart we had to raise our hand and we would be taken outside by an attendant as smarting indicated a leak in the gas-mask.

Every city and town had air-raid sirens. In the Valley the sirens were manned around the clock by the local fire-brigades. We practiced a drill at school that required all the classes to form up in an orderly manner and march to the air-raid shelter in an orderly manner and without panic. By 1943 and after most of the air-raids had stopped the shelters in our area fell into disuse. Many were still there after the war and we took one over for a gang-hut. Other enterprising persons used them as garden sheds and storage while some young lovers found them a convenient place to be private.

Toys in wartime....

It would be very difficult for parents of today to contemplate life without being able to buy toys for their children; yet children in the Valley born during the war years had to survive without such things as toys, bicycles, sweets and comics. It's not that parents were too poor to buy them, it was just the simple fact that there were no toys available to buy as all the materials used for making such things were all prioritised for the war effort.

Yet we survived without them and in the long term were probably better off for it as it made us understand even at our young age that there were priorities in life. However, we still looked forward to Christmas and continued to ask Father Christmas to bring us things we knew we were not going to get. On Christmas morning we would run eagerly downstairs to see if Father Christmas had left us anything, but we knew it was the war that was stopping him from getting through to us. I've often wondered since how heartbreaking it must have been for parents to see the hope and belief in their children's eyes, only to see the disappointment when there was little for them under the Christmas tree. Mum and Dad did their best to make up for the absence of toys and they always managed to put together a few surprises. Somehow they always managed to get hold of some chocolates and an orange; a big shiny red apple and sometimes a new sixpenny piece or a three penny-bit.

Britain had been at war for five years before my brother and I received our first toy; I was nine and Raymond eleven. Two doors up the street from where we lived was the Veal family. Mr Veal (Alf) dabbled in photography. Unknown to us Dad had negotiated with Mr Veal to make us both a toy aeroplane for Christmas. On Christmas morning we dashed downstairs as usual and were amazed to find toys among our presents. Raymond got a Lancaster bomber and I got a Wellington bomber. I can't begin to explain the exhilaration I felt at receiving such a gift, and although we had passed the stage of believing in Father Christmas, we almost believed that Santa had got through at last.

Christmas day......during the war....

Although there were no toys, Mum and dad always managed to make Christmas special for us. The first treat would be a full cooked breakfast with bacon and one whole fried egg (this was a special treat as due to rationing we usually only had one half egg a week) with fried tomatoes and toast. Christmas lunch would be delayed until late afternoon and was the family event of the year. Dad would usually arrive home from work on Christmas Eve with two large hens (turkeys only existed in story books and the imagination) and a big piece of pork. We would sit down with Mum and pull the feathers off the hens and be disgusted when she pulled the innards out. Lunch was a magnificent feast of roast meats, roast potatoes and vegetables from Dad's allotment and homemade stuffing. All followed with Mum's homemade Christmas pudding and custard.

Christmas day was the only day Dad would allow beer in the house but as a special treat he would allow the older brothers to bring in one case of beer. Mum and Dad would indulge in a glass of sherry and the younger kids would have glasses of tizer and dandelion and burdock. After the Christmas feast and the table had been cleared we would play a card game called 'finding the lady' and as with beer Dad only allowed card games to be played once a year and after Christmas lunch. At this time Mum would produce boxes of dates and dishes of peanuts and as a special treat we were allowed to stay-up late.

Not having toys for Christmas was a huge disappointment but Mum and Dad did everything they could to give us a good Christmas and must have spent a lot of time planning and saving money and food to make Christmas special.

War-time rationing....

I was four years-old when WW2 started and along with millions of other British children we had to suffer the severe restrictions of food rationing which the government had to introduce to ensure the equitable spread of the limited amount of food available. Although buying food with ration coupons was an irksome job, we were never allowed to forget that thousands of men and women were sacrificing their lives to bring home the convoys of ships to keep us fed and save us from starving.

My own children tend to ridicule me when I reminisce (perhaps too often) that I was fourteen before I had my first banana. I don't know how they did it, but every Christmas on the last day of school before the holiday we would receive a shiny red apple as a gift from the Canadian government

I often wonder how children today would cope without sweets and how much better off they would be without them. We were allowed a small number of sweet coupons, but the shops rarely had any to sell. It was a few years after the war ended before sweets occasionally become available. When a shop did receive supplies word would spread rapidly and there would be mad long dash to join the queue before stocks ran out.

Ration books were issued to every man, woman and child. There were different books for things like meat, eggs, fats, cheese, bacon, sugar, tea, sweets and clothing. My mother God bless her soul was illiterate (illiteracy was still common in many of the early miners' families) and while she would often ask us to explain details to her she still managed the ration books for all the family. She did so well that although things were scarce we never went short and she would occasionally help desperate neighbours who had been careless in the management of their coupons.

The Barnsley British Co-operative Society (BBCS) was very strong in the Valley and one of the chores for my brothers and I was to wheel our barrow to the High Street co-op at the top of Pearson's Field and opposite Burrow's garage, every Friday after school to collect the weekly food rations. Mum would have called at the shop earlier in the day to place her order and deposit the ration coupons. When we got home with the barrow, Mum would separate what was for immediate use and what went into the locked wooden chest at the foot of her bed which contained her reserves and items for special events such as Christmas and Easter.

The severest rationing was on meat. Miners such as my three brothers were allocated extra coupons because of the strenuous nature of their work underground that was vital to the war effort. Most of the meat ration went on sausages for Dad and my brothers, then what was left of the meat ration was used to make stew which Mum would serve with her fantastic Yorkshire puddings. We never had chips and all our potatoes were boiled, mashed, roasted in the oven or cut-up with vegetables to make ash. It was a long time after the war ended before Mum was able to buy a joint of beef to roast and make roast beef and Yorkshire puddings. Today there are few women who can make Yorkshire puddings the way miners' wives could, before and after the war. For anybody to believe that packets of Yorkshire puddings that can be purchased from supermarkets can be compared with home-made puddings is an illusion.

The renewal of clothing was a major problem as the coupon ration was very small due to the big demand for clothing from the armed-forces. But Mum dealt with the problem as usual and we were never reduced to rags as some unfortunates were. Being a large family there was scarcely two years between our ages and consequently hand-downs helped to ensure that every item of clothing purchased was passed down several times before it eventually expired. My brothers and I were limited to one new suit a year with my sisters getting a new coat and a frock. Mum in her usual competent way always managed to combine the buying of new clothes with the annual 'divi', money she received from the co-op on her purchases. The declaration of the annual 'divi' was always an eagerly awaited event in the Valley. As Mum was a big spender at the co-op with having a large family, she always accrued enough in 'divi' to pay off her outstanding credit account and still have enough left over to pay for the annual renewal of our clothing.

New clothes were always purchased for Whitsuntide so that we could show off our new clothes as we paraded around the town at the Whitsuntide Walk which would finish with the crowning of a Whitsuntide queen on the feastfield. As the parade passed the top of our street (Hawson Street) all the neighbours would turn out to watch the parade and Mum would be right there at the front positively beaming with pride at the sight of her children parading in their new clothes. After Whitsuntide, our previous Sunday best became school only clothes and our previous school clothes were used for playing time and doing household jobs.

Rationing helped Britons to survive the war but many of the nation's children paid a price when their families failed to manage their affairs and were often without bread and other essential foods. Some mother's would beg BU's (bread units used for rationing bread) from Mum to feed their hungry children and I never saw her refuse. Cases of rickets and malnutrition were high and normal physical growth for many children was stunted for many years. Even after the end of war it took several years before people were able to obtain sufficient food for nutrition and good health. Food rationing was only finally brought to an end in 1954....nine years after the end of the war.

The Barnsley British Co-operative Society (BBCS)....

The BBCS was born in the Tinker's Temperance Hall, May Day Green, Barnsley in 1860, when a small group of men decided it would be a good idea to form a Co-operative Society. They later joined the Barnsley Flour Society and with others agreed to make a subscription of one shilling a-week from the 3rd August 1861. By February 1862 subscriptions had reached £30 and the committee decided they had enough funds to start a selling operation.

The first BBCS shop in the Valley was opened in Market Street, Barnsley on the 13th March 1862 and the first customer to step into the shop was a Mr Jos Fish, a picture-framer, who purchased two pounds of soap. Business started to grow so that by the end of the first quarter sales had reached £550.13.6d and members contributions were £48.17.2d. A dividend of one shilling in the pound was declared. Sales continued to increase to the extent that the committee had to look for bigger premises and a decision was taken to move to new larger premises in Wellington Street. Membership continued to grow and the following year a 'divi' of 1s.3d was declared.

Business at the BBCS continued to grow and by 1869 six new shops had been opened. Also in 1969 the Society built its own flour mill to supply its increasing number of shops. Membership continued to increase and by 1887 exceeded 10 000 enabling the Society to expand its business into butchery, bakery and drapery followed in 1891 with boots and shoes, tailoring, furnishing and in 1893 the Society purchased a mineral water manufacturing business. New branches continued to be opened so that by 1900 sales exceeded £650 000 with profits of over £100 000, while membership had increased to 20 000.

The BBCS continued to trade throughout the difficult years of WW1 and was instrumental in assisting bereaved families of employees and society members. Although the BBCS continued to achieve good results it had to contend with a downturn during the 1926 strike as many of its customers were miners who had no wages for over a year. But the business was strong and able to survive while still assisting miners and their families. The BBCS became an integral part in the lives of people in the Valley. The provision of groceries and other essential goods at competitive prices along with the highly valued pay back 'divi' was highly valued by all sections of the working-class in the Valley.

The Second World War with food and clothing rationed was another great test for the BBCS as many male employees were called-up for the war and sales became restricted as the government rationed the small amounts of food that became available. The end of the war was a turning point in the fortunes of the society. Food rationing did not officially end until 1954 but already an even greater threat was looming for the society. In 1953 the new concept of self-service stores burst onto the scene and immediately began making inroads into the society's business. The directors of the BBCS were mostly Labour politicians and trade union officials and where the society should have been at the forefront of the change in retailing, they failed to respond.

The rot on a previously successful business set-in and gradually shops started to close and the 'divi' continued to fall. The failure of the directors to recruit new senior management capable of establishing the BBCS in the new highly competitive retail environment resulted in a continuous fall in sales and shop closures throughout the Valley. Few co-op shops are around today to remind us of the glory days of the BBCS and the outstanding service they gave to the Valley, often in very difficult times and over so many years.

My heritage....

I was born in the Valley on the 8th December 1935, just nine years after the 1926 strike and four years before the start of WW2, both events having a big impact on my life. I was the third youngest in a family of thirteen children and grew to adulthood at the family home in 18 Hawson Street Wombwell, South Yorkshire in the Dearne Valley. My grandparents on my mother's side are believed to have been among the many families desperate for employment that migrated to the Yorkshire coalfields. The only relative I have been able to connect to is my Uncle Jack who lived with my grandparents in Smith Street, Low Valley, Darfield. Uncle Jack had gained a reputation as an amateur boxer before joining his mates in volunteering for service in Kitchener's Army and was killed in action in France in December 1917.

My father, Fred Hargreaves, who originated from Salford in Lancashire was orphaned as a teenager and spent his early adult years as a stoker in the Merchant Navy. On the outbreak of WW1 he joined the Royal Navy and had the distinction of being sunk twice; one ship striking a mine and the other being sunk by a German submarine. When the war ended he had no home to go to so one of his pals persuaded him to go home with him to Darfield. As a former stoker he was quickly able to obtain employment as a boiler-fireman at Houghton Main Colliery. Shortly after he met and married my mother Rose Hanna Smith who was employed as a domestic at the George Hotel, Low Valley, Darfield.

Mum and Dad had a large family even by the standards of the time, but no child could have wished for more loving and caring parents. Even during the difficult war years and rationing, we never went hungry and were always adequately clothed, even if trousers and frocks were sometimes held together with large patches.

At various times members of the family moved to Canada, Australia and South Africa. My sister Mona served in the Women's Royal Army Corps throughout WW2 and my late brother Henry did three years duty with the Royal Artillery in Palestine shortly after the war. My brothers Raymond, Malcolm and myself all served national service in the armed-forces. Raymond served in the Royal Air Force; Malcolm in the Royal Artillery while I served in the infantry with the 1st Bn. The Duke of Wellington's Regiment. One benefit of large families is that they can offer more services to the state when it is required.

Slums, outside toilets.... ....bed-bugs and chamber pots....

The family accommodation in Hawson Street was a terraced slum, one of many in the Valley that were built on the cheap by mine-owners to house thousands of families flooding into the area to work at the mines. Our house in a street of over 90 terraced slums consisted of two downstairs rooms, two upstairs rooms, an attic and a coal cellar. All the rooms were very small in size. One of the downstairs rooms was the kitchen which had a fire-place with a coal heated cooking-range that heated a tank on the left side to provide hot water, an oven on the right side and two pan holders that could be moved over the fire. Also in the kitchen was a stone sink with only a cold-water tap and gas mantle lighting in the ceiling. Lighting in the other rooms was only by candlelight. The second downstairs room was a living-room with a small coal-fireplace where we would sit around in the evenings to listen to the radio. Underneath the ground floor rooms was a cellar where one half was for coal storage and the other half acted as cold storage as even in summer months Mum was still able to store perishable items such as milk, veggies and bread which had to be baked then stored in large quantities. One of my major tasks as a younger member of the household was to keep two buckets of coal ready for use at the top of the cellar steps. I hated having to go into the dark cellar as there was only a little light from an outside grate and I had to struggle to carry the full buckets up the cellar steps.

The two upstairs rooms were bedroom accommodation for Mum and Dad and in the second room were too very large beds that just about took all the available space. My sisters slept in one bed while my brothers and I slept in the other. Our older brothers slept in two beds squeezed into the attic. At times eleven people were living, sleeping and eating in that tiny house. When my sister Mona came home on army leave she had to sleep in the downstairs room.

One of the worst discomforts we had to suffer was the outside lavatory across the yard. Unless you have experienced having to trudge across a yard in mid-winter at night to sit in a freezing toilet and quite often having to wait in a queue to get there, then you have never experienced discomfort. To add to the misery, the lavatory cistern would often freeze solid in winter entailing additional trips across a slippery yard with buckets of water to flush the toilet.

We could only afford one newspaper (The Daily Herald) which besides bringing us news of the war also provided the family with toilet paper. After Dad had finished reading the paper Mum would cut the pages into small squares and stick them on a nail behind the lavatory door. Anybody using the paper excessively elicited the wrath of the entire family. Inevitably, there would at times be a queue for the lavatory, especially at week-ends when all the family were at home. Sometimes serious arguments broke out as to whose turn it was next with Mum having to intervene and separate a pair trying to settle the issue with fists. How Mum kept her sanity in the midst of all the mayhem beggars understanding.

The houses down Hawson Street, as in most of the Valley, had been thrown-up as cheaply as possible to save the mine-owners profits and given the harsh winter conditions in those years, the walls were constantly damp. Mum made valiant attempts to contain the damp by papering the walls with cheap wallpaper then painting over with distemper (a cheap paint) but given the conditions in a small overcrowded bedroom, the walls were continually invaded with bugs. Dad made many complaints about the damp to the council's public-health officer but nothing was achieved as the council had long ago concluded that the only answer was to demolish the houses, but unfortunately due to the war they were unable to build new houses to replace them.

Chamber pots were a necessity. The younger children were always in bed by 8pm and the need to stay in bed until 7am the next morning (giving Mum time to get older siblings off to work) meant that young bladders that couldn't get out of bed to go across the yard had to be released. Quite often the pot would be full but God help anybody who caused an overflow.

Wash day was always on a Wednesday with Mum facing a mountain of clothes and bedding to wash with only a basic tub with rubbing-board and an old two roller mangle for squeezing out the water before hanging the wash out to dry. I hated wash day because I had to spend my lunchtime break from school turning the mangle as Mum fed the washing into the rollers. If you can imagine the amount of washing and ironing requirement for eleven people that had to take place every week, regardless of the weather for drying, then you can appreciate the size of the task. When the weather was bad, bed sheets and clothes would be strung out on washing-lines in both downstairs rooms. Mum would keep the fire stoked up to speed up the drying process causing the house to be full of steam.

In spite of their poverty Hawson Street housewives took a great pride in showing-off the condition of their bed sheets on the washing-lines strung across their back-yard. The London and North Eastern Railway (LNER) ran across the bottom of the street and the steam engines belched clouds of soot, but on Wednesdays the train drivers knowing it was wash day would always toot a loud warning as they approached Hawson Street; the women would then drop everything and dash out into the back yard to drag the washing from their lines until the train had passed.

Bathing, cooking, baking and gas-light....

It would seem to be impossible for eleven people living in slum housing to be able to keep clean and free from disease, yet my parents ensured that our clothes were always clean and that the smaller children washed daily and had a bath in a tin bath in front of the coal-fire every Saturday night so that we would be clean for Sunday school the next day. Some families in the street were not able to do so, for whatever reason, consequently skin diseases such as 'impetigo' and 'head nits' were rampant. Once every week Mum would sit down with a bowl of vinegar and a 'nit' comb and give our hair a thorough cleansing; as a result we were never picked-out by school nurses for having 'nits' and my mother's reputation for good childcare by teachers and school nurses was enhanced even further.

My Mum's day would start at 4.30am every week day and sometimes over week-ends when Dad was on week-end duty. She would be out of bed to make the fire and pack snap-tins for the older brothers before they went to work on day shift. After doing various chores such as patching school clothes and darning, she would get the older sisters out of bed, breakfast them and see them off to work. Next she would get us younger kids out of bed and stand over us while we washed our hands and face and polished our school shoes. Our breakfast often coincided with Dad arriving home in the morning from night-shift and Mum would have his breakfast ready. After dosing us with generous helpings of cod-liver-oil and malt and seeing us off to school, Mum would then clear all the breakfast things away and make a start on her many other chores such as cleaning and the daily baking. Baking was an important daily task for Mum as shop bread was very expensive and as bread was rationed Mum used all her BU's (bread coupons) to buy flour and was then able to bake enough bread to keep us all well fed. She somehow always managed to have some BU's spare to help neighbours who would come to her begging for help after being unable to control their ration coupons and had no bread for their children. The only cooking facilities Mum had was the coal fire and oven. How she was able to cook so many meals and bake the mountain of bread the family needed was incredible. Although fruit was rationed there always seemed to be a plentiful supply of damsons with which Mum made stocks of jam to avoid having to use ration coupons to buy jam from the shops.

How Mum managed to cook the constant stream of meals necessary to feed and sustain such a large family is nothing short of a miracle. Besides the mountain of bread she baked daily, once every week she would bake jam tarts for Sunday tea and fruit duff made from suet pudding and raisins. A great favourite for us was the dumplings she made with vegetables and thick gravy while her rabbit pie was out of this world. Most meals were made to fill stomachs and Mum never failed to do so.

I've often wondered why rabbit is so little used for meals today and particularly in poor countries. Rabbits breed very fast and are cheap to feed. During the war years almost every house in our street had a rabbit hutch outside the back door. When the rabbits had been made into meals, the women would select the best skins to make gloves for winter and leggings to wrap around their ankles. Besides making an extremely nutritious meal nothing from the rabbit was wasted.

Saturday night was bath night in a tin bath in front of the fire which was convenient for Mum to ladle hot water from the boiler after we had carried buckets of cold water from the kitchen tap. My sisters always had the privilege of going first while the boys would sit and listen to the radio. When Mum had finished the girls she would then set about us boys and one by one give us a good scrub. Although it was only one bath a week she made sure it was a good one.

In my younger days in the Valley, gas lighting was the only means of household lighting other than a candle. It was a most unpleasant method and on entering a house one was always hit with the smell of gas. Light was provided via a small, flimsy gas-mantle that would always choose to wear out at the most inconvenient time, such as night time which would involve a scramble for matches and a candle to provide light to change the gas-mantle.

Gas street lighting in my home town of Wombwell was first introduced around 1870 and was still the main means of domestic lighting after the end of the war. In Hawson Street the street gas light was a meeting point where the lads and lasses would gather after having had their tea and been released from household chores. Although my friends and I were no angels, the street lights were never vandalised. I often wonder how long they would have lasted if exposed to some of the youth today.

Household duties....

With a large family cramped into such small accommodation, good organisation was essential and right at the top of the management pile was my Mum who could neither read nor write. Although she had to rule with a rod of iron to keep order, she never lost her motherly tenderness and was always on hand to give comfort and love when needed.

Everybody was allocated jobs, even Dad who besides working a three shift cycle where he was in charge of the men stoking the colliery boilers, was responsible for the garden allotment and producing lots of vegetables to help the family budget and keep us all healthy at times of acute shortages. Although Mum was responsible for the clothing ration books, Dad had to always ensure we always had leak proof footwear and didn't go to school with holes in our shoes like a lot of kids. To take the strain off the clothing allowance and to avoid buying new shoes too often, he would buy a large piece of leather to repair our shoes from some chap at the mine. Our shoes must have lasted three or four times longer than most kids as Mum would make us polish our shoes every morning to help preserve the tops. When repairs were needed Dad would sit down on the floor with his 'hobbin-foot' (a tool that was used to repair different size shoes) and cut the leather to the size of our feet and then nail to the sole of the shoe to secure, extending the life of our shoes for a few more months.

Our older brothers didn't have many extra jobs as their responsibility was to be at work every day and bring the money home. Sometimes at week-ends they would go shooting and on a good day would return with rabbits which helped the strain on the meat ration. My sisters had to help Mum with the washing, ironing and cleaning, but at times there would be a real rumpus such as only women could make; usually over who does what and who hadn't done that. However Mum always managed to keep the situation under control and made sure the jobs got done.

My younger brothers and I had the job of keeping the home fires burning, a job we disliked as it meant trips down the dark cellar and a climb back up the steps with a heavy bucket of coal. As a mine employee Dad was allowed one ton of free coal every month as part of his wages and had only to pay a delivery charge. The home-coal delivery truck would deposit the coal as near as possible to our cellar grate on the pavement outside the house. We dreaded arriving home from school to find a ton of coal waiting for us and which meant we had to shovel the coal down the grate and into the cellar before we could have our tea and go out to the gang.

One duty my brothers and I disliked intensely was 'horse-mucking'. Dad's allotment was always in intensive use to be able to feed a large family and required a lot of compost, the essential component being horse droppings of which we were required to collect two barrow-loads every week. This was one chore we had that our mates didn't have to do because their Dad's didn't have an allotment, but they would always come with us as the gang couldn't function if we weren't there. It was fortunate for us that most of the council's motor vehicles had been taken away by the government for war duty and replaced with big Shire-horses. We would wheel our barrow along the streets we knew the council carts used and collected the horse droppings. Sometimes when the supply was small we would follow a horse and cart hoping for a dropping.

Dad's compost heap was the envy of all the other allotment holders which he achieved in spite of working and supervising a demanding three-cycle shift in the colliery boiler-room. His production of new potatoes, cabbages, sprouts and carrots was quite substantial. A large patch of rhubarb enabled Mum to make a lot of rhubarb pies which we ate with homemade hot custard. A patch of mint flavoured many of our dinners. During the war the government ran a big 'Dig for Victory' campaign to encourage people to grow as much of their own food as possible and many turned their flower gardens into vegetable patches, but unfortunately there were also those who couldn't be bothered to dig.

Although there were disagreements and even fights among the younger end of the family, we stuck to our jobs and all helped the family to have a reasonably comfortable life. Looking back as I often do, I marvel at the way my parents were able to organise our lives and ensured we grew-up healthy, clean and in spite of food rationing, well fed. Some of my mates were not so lucky and would often go home from school to a bread and dripping tea and seldom had a hot meal.

Home entertainment....

During the 1940's the main source of family entertainment in the Valley was the radio. Firstly, the radio was essential to keep the public informed on the progress of the war and a means of communication from the government to the people. Secondly, the radio provided the cheapest means of entertainment for the working-class.

I still remember many of the radio programmes with great affection for the happiness they brought to us during the very difficult and unpleasant war years. Most nights the family would gather around the radio in the sitting-room with only candle light (to save money on gas) listening to programmes such as 'Valentine Dyall and the man in Black', a mystery thriller that had us kids shivering and shaking. Sunday afternoon was always special with the serialisation of 'King Solomon's Mines'. I would run home from school every day to make sure I didn't miss the ten minute daily serialisation of 'Dick Barton-Special Agent' with his pals, Snowy and Jock. Tommy Handley's 'ITMA' was also a great favourite as was 'Workers' Playtime' and many other comedy and music programmes such as 'Manitoban' and his orchestra.

Although the family only had money to spend on essential items such as food and clothing, when the war ended and things got a little better Mum would place an order for weekly comics for us such as the, Dandy, Beano, Comic-Cuts and later Dan Dare the first space adventure comic. Other budgeted leisure activities were one visit a-week to the cinema, usually the Saturday morning matinee at the Pav (Pavilion cinema) and one visit a-week to Wombwell swimming baths (where we also took advantage of using the showers) which could be exchanged for another cinema visit during the winter months when the baths was converted to a dance hall. Mum and Dad only managed a cinema visit (which was the extent of their social life as Dad never frequented pubs) once every three weeks when Dad's three shift cycle dropped on the day shift.

Every Sunday afternoon was a special event. Older brothers and sisters would bring their girl-friends and boy-friends and it was always like a big party. What was very special for me was that tea always concluded with Mum's home baked jam tarts and on special occasions she would bake a chocolate cake with the most fantastic butter cream. The kitchen was the main eating area (the only area) and the furniture consisted of a huge dresser (sideboard) with the middle drawers pulled out which with the use of cushions provided four extra seats down one side of the table; somehow ten of us could be seated around the table at one time. When there were extra visitors there would be two sittings with Mum and Dad and the adults going first and us kids waiting for the second sitting, but Mum always made sure we never lost out and received exactly the same as the first sitting.

The front ground floor room was always referred to as 'the room', which I suppose would in larger houses be described as the sitting-room. This was the social area of the house with two easy chairs and a large sofa and where the radio was located. There was a small fire-grate and Mum would allow us to make a fire on cold winter Sundays. Not that we were ever short of coal as our coal cellar was always full with the free coal supplied to colliery employees, but Mum and Dad had long memories of many shortages during strikes and were determined we would never go short in the event of a bad winter or a long strike. These were special times for us huddled around the fire on a cold Sunday night listening to Mantovani and his orchestra on the radio. Just after the war my older brothers were able to buy a record player and we played the one record 'Those riders in the Sky', endlessly.

Additional to everything else that had to be squashed into the small kitchen was four bicycles as Dad and three older brothers all cycled to Houghton Main colliery. This would have been a big saving for them on bus fares but must have been very unpleasant during the winter months. The bicycles were too important and expensive to be left to the elements outside the house. I recall on several occasions seeing Dad arrive home from night-shift completely covered in snow. It must have taken a determined and committed man to cycle almost six miles home in the snow, yet I never heard Dad complain and he was turned 55 years-of-age before he gave up cycling to work in favour of the bus and passed his bicycle on to me.

Mum and Dad were not churchgoers but Mum would always make us attend Sunday school and she would always attend the annual anniversary at Park Street chapel at the top of our street to see us sat on the stage in our Sunday best and receiving our book prizes for good attendance. The only time Dad ever attended church was when there was a marriage in the family, but our attendance at Sunday school was compulsory.

Seaside trips....

During the war years the coastline was heavily defended and the beaches mined as it was possible for German invaders to land on any of the many beaches. As youngsters we went through the war years never having seen the sea and never having been on a holiday, which were things we could only dream about. Shortly after the end of the war military defences were removed and the beaches cleared of mines allowing the public access to the beaches again.

As one war year passed on into another in the Valley, there were two things we youngsters craved for; one was to see and eat a banana and the other was to see the sea. My first trip to the seaside came when the local Working Men's' Club organised a day trip to the seaside at Bridlington for members' children when the war ended. It was a day I will never forget. Mum came along with me, two brothers and two of my sisters. That morning we made our way to the railway station with great excitement as this was also our very first ride on a train. At the station we were met by club officials who gave Mum seven shillings and sixpence for each one of us (a fortune to us) a packet of sandwiches and some fruit to eat on the train and a name tag just in case we got lost in Bridlington.

As the train pulled away from the station we leaned out of the windows cheering wildly and waving to the hundreds of people who had come to see us off. When we arrived in Bridlington there was no sun and the sky was overcast, but that didn't deter us in the least. Although it was cold we found a place on the beach and paddled excitedly in the sea until Mum called us for lunch. She had prepared a lunch of spam sandwiches, boiled eggs and tomatoes, for which she must have dug deep into the family ration reserves. After lunch we had donkey rides and then headed towards 'Wonderland' where there was such things as dodgem cars and ghost rains, things we had never imagined before. Mum allowed us to spend 2/6d, but ever prudent, she kept the rest for us to deposit in our school savings account.

After 'Wonderland' there was just enough time left to visit the 'rock shops' that sold all kinds of variations of seaside rock that we had heard of but had never seen and where sweet rationing (still in force) did not seem to apply. We were allowed to stock-up enough rock to last several weeks which wouldn't have done our teeth much good but that didn't concern us at the time. After years of sweets deprivation sticks of sticky rock were the ultimate luxury that Mum didn't deny us. I'm not sure if the tradition of buying rock at the seaside still continues as most parents today would be reluctant to allow their children to grind their teeth on hard rock because of the damage it would do to their teeth. The school dental service would however have taken a dim of view of children chewing rock as they were already busy yanking teeth out of many children due to food rationing and malnutrition.

The return journey home was much quieter than when we left Wombwell in the morning. After an adventure packed day and the exposure to sea air, most of us fell asleep as the train chugged its way back to Wombwell. When we arrived back at the station the platform was filled with hundreds of fathers waiting to welcome their children back from their first adventure at the seaside and many had to carry their sleeping children home. It was a day that I will never forget.

Day trips to the seaside became very popular with most streets organising trips, as also did many clubs and pubs. For many mine workers' families in the Valley a full week holiday at the sea was still a long way away; a far cry from the continental holidays that so many take today.

Cinemas and roller-rinks....

Cinemas in the Valley were very popular during and after the war. Most days, no matter what film was showing there would be queues outside the Empire and Pavilion cinemas in Wombwell. There were two shows every night, the first at 5pm and the second at 7.30pm. The second-house, as it was called, was the most popular and mostly used by adults while the first house was mostly for young people and pensioners who got a discount and took the pressure off the second-house.

The Empire was opposite where I lived in Hawson Street. It was the most popular as it had an elitist air about it and had an upper-circle. The manager, a Mr Nash, always wore a tuxedo and black bow-tie and looked very important and superior. Saturday night was an important social event at the Empire even if there was only a third rate film showing. Reservations were necessary for the second-house with a big demand for seats in the circle that were a much higher price than the stalls.

There was an element of snobbery about the Empire considering it was in a small mining town. My older brothers, sisters and friends wouldn't go on a Saturday night if they failed to get seat reservations in the circle. There were three entrances to the cinema proper and as the patrons entered through the front doors, attendants would inspect the colour of their tickets and direct them to the respective entrance; front stalls to the right, back stall to the middle and circle patrons to the left and all watched over by an imperious Mr Nash. Many of Wombwell's elite would only ever be seen being directed to the left.

The front part of the stalls was the cheapest but caused a pain in the neck as there was very little elevation in the stalls and it was a matter of luck if you got a seat behind a big person blocking a view of the screen. Smoking was also a hazard as many people smoked in those days and it was extremely unpleasant being surrounded by a huge smug of smoke and the unpleasant smell from often overflowing ash trays.

Many shows were often preceded by a sing-along accompanied by an organ. Pathe news programmes were very popular as it was the only visual means to see how the war was progressing around the world. Always at the end of a show the national anthem would be played and everybody would stand until the last note was played.

Roller skating was very popular during and after the war at a rink in Low Valley (a village in a Valley on the low side of Darfield that was on a hill) and next to a soccer ground where I regularly as a boy watched Mark Jones (one of our local lads) who at the time was playing for Don and Dearne boys before being selected for Manchester United. Mark later became an English international player but tragically died in the Munich air-crash.

Street gangs....

To mention the word 'gangs' immediately strikes fear in the minds of many. It pictures violence, robbery, drugs, rape and even murder, so I was a little reluctant to discuss street gangs until I realised it was important to make comparison with how we lived our lives in the slums of the Valley in far worse circumstances than many deprived youngsters of today.

I suppose it's true to say that I was born into a gang dynasty. My older brothers all belonged to the Hawson Street gang and as they grew older and into employment and moved away, we younger brothers took their place. The males in my family had always been in the upper echelon of the gang so the younger brothers enjoyed a lot of protection and favouritism.

The Hawson Street gang was not just a motley collection of youths as the structure was highly organised and disciplined. Gang meetings took place most nights in the Hawson Street air-raid shelter by candlelight. All members were allowed to express an opinion, but decisions once made were written in blood. There were three sections in the gang – the 'top-enders' (who lived at the top of the street) were the elite and gang bosses, while the 'middle-streeters' were closely allied to the 'top-enders' and the 'bottom-enders' were the serfs who were allowed to assist the gang when required such as helping in gang fights and collecting wood for bonfires.

For some reason I never fully understood, the 'top-enders' were the more well-off residents in the street with the degree of affluence declining as one descended down the street. If a 'bottom-ender' passed a 'top-ender' on his way down the street he would get a courtesy thump. We really gave those people a hard time and consequently when we needed their assistance they would jump. For some strange reason all the best looking girls came from the 'bottom-enders' and most of them had boy friend's from the 'top-enders'. As I grew older I developed a strong friendship with two guys who were 'bottom-enders' which lasted until we left school to work at different coal mines. Shortly after I completed National Service and working as a trainee-manager, one former 'bottom-ender' asked me to be best-man at his wedding.

There were numerous street gangs in Wombwell; the 'Hawson Streeters' (my street) was mostly regarded as the top gang, a position that was constantly challenged and resulted in many bloody gang fights. The other gangs were the Ship Crofters, King's Roaders, Barnsley Roaders, Blythe Streeters, Station Laners, Alma Streeters, Broomhillers and some lesser gangs with virtually every street having a gang. The strange thing was that during school time no gang rules applied and everybody could move around the town with no problem. Another truce was applied to Saturday and Sunday because there was a morning and afternoon cinema matinee on Saturday and because on Sunday most of us went to Sunday school. But outside these times one would only trespass into another street with plenty of back-up.

The biggest fight was always when the annual fair came to town at the feast field across the road from King's Road school on the north side and across the road from Hawson Street on the south side. The gangs would assemble at the feastfield on the day before the fair opened. Alliances would be made between several gangs as the main objective of the fight was to push the Hawson Streeters out of the feastfield and across the road into Hawson Street. The Hawson Streeters however would never make any alliance with any other gang and we were often outnumbered.

This was a fight 'for turf' in more sense than one as it was fought almost entirely with 'grass-sods' (clumps of grass pulled from the ground and full of soil). To be the recipient of a grass-sod thrown at full force was an extremely unpleasant experience. The opposing gangs would do their best to push us back across the road and into Hawson Street, but we had honour to maintain, handed down from brother to brother and there was no way we could allow any gang to beat us. Consequently, Park Street (the main road through Wombwell) and separating the feastfield and Hawson Street was our last line of defence. At times the fighting was so fierce that the road would be blocked and the traffic stopped as scores of youths beat each other silly with grass sods, cheered on by a large crowd. The fight would start shortly after school and everybody had had time to go home for tea, then continued until the light started to fail when almost by signal the fighting would stop and everybody would go home to wash dirt out of their eyes and nurse their bruised bodies and be ready for school the next morning. We were never beaten and no other gang member ever put his foot into Hawson Street.

The canal bank....

The Dearne and Dove canal that flowed across the bottom of Hawson Street had been extremely important in the development of industry in the Valley, but as industry declined it became totally disused and a receptacle for rubbish and a convenient place to dispose of unwanted dogs and cats. Across the canal at the bottom of the street was the local gas-works and further back the LNER railway line. A footpath ran parallel with the canal all the way to Broomhill Bridge passing a half submerged coal barge that was the only reminder of earlier days. On the railway side of the footpath hedged by trees and shrubs (where the gang did most of its training) were fields used by a local farmer (Charlesworth) to graze his cattle and could be accessed from Hawson Street over the canal by a dilapidated bridge. This bridge was strategic for the Hawson Streeters as it provided an escape route in case we were ever overwhelmed in battle. Only two planks on the bridge were passable so on the few occasions we had to make a strategic retreat across the bridge, we could easily defend ourselves as the enemy would have to cross the bridge in single file and would have taken a ducking in the canal for their foolishness. Access to the bridge was at the top of the hill where most of our activities took place and where we had a good view of any invaders coming from Broomhill. At the bottom of the hill was level ground where we played cricket and football. Further on towards the railway line was long grass which was convenient for a little female dalliance when the opportunity presented itself.

The canal bank was the scene of some bloody battles as we armed ourselves with bows and arrows and made wooden swords. On some occasions as many as a hundred kids from the camps of the Hawson Streeters and the Broomhillers would be armed to the teeth and facing each other. Hawson Streeters always had the advantage as we camped at the top of the hill. We would wait until the enemy shouted 'charge' and started running up the hill, then our leader would also shout charge. The added momentum of charging downhill gave us weight advantage, then as the two sides clashed all hell would let loose until one side, usually the Broomhillers, would break off and run away with us in hot pursuit, catching those who couldn't run fast enough and taking prisoners. Prisoners were usually held until the end of the day and were well treated the only punishment was being relieved of their weapons.

Nobody ever had to go to hospital or be treated by a doctor. No parents ever complained and nobody ever attempted to stop the fights. Quite often word would get around and a crowd would gather on the footpath to watch the battle and cheer the lads on. The next day would see us playing conkers with each other in the school playground or playing in the same football and cricket teams. I sometimes try to compare our young lives and adventures with what youngsters do today and I feel it is sad they never had the chance to experience the comradeship, loyalty and trust that we enjoyed with our mates.

Some of the boys would later be called for National Service in the armed-forces and would probably have served in such places as Burma, Korea, Western Germany, Gibraltar, Kenya, Hong Kong and Cyprus. Without any doubt their early experiences of life would have been an asset to them when it was needed.

The canal bank was a popular place for young lovers wanting to be alone as there was little privacy back in the streets. It was also a haven for us kids, being the nearest thing we could consider as countryside, even though the canal was badly polluted. The gas-works smelled badly and there was non-stop pollution from steam trains passing through Wombwell's 'bottom station' trailing long lines of coal wagons to and from the collieries. But it was our canal bank and long after the gas-works disappeared it was still a popular place to take a walk.

The canal was eventually filled-in to make way for a badly needed town by-pass, but for me the continuous drone of cars and heavy vehicles will never drown the cries of boys charging manfully into battle. The canal will always have a special place in my memories of the Valley.

The Church, Chapels and the Salvation Army....

As youngsters, the religious organisations in the Valley played a large part in our lives as there were few recreational facilities. While we attended the more austere chapels, we would stand in awe and watch the Church Lad's Brigade parading with their bugles and drums and dressed in their very smart and expensive uniforms. Membership of the brigade was for the children of the more affluent of Wombwell society. Today, the local brigades consist mostly of girls, a sure reminder of the gender reversal that is crippling the male role in British society that could have serious consequences for the future.

The Methodist Chapels were mostly for us poor kids from the slums and a great job they did. Park Street Methodist Chapel (just around the corner from the top of Hawson Street) had two chapels on the opposite sides of Park Street. One was situated next to Guest's undertakers at the top of Hawson Street and was mostly used as a Sunday school and for special events. The one across the road situated between the police-station and the Conservative Club was for adult services and had a splendid organ. Mum always made us attend both morning and afternoon sessions of Sunday school.

The Park Street chapel had a very vibrant and active Sunday school and it indicates something of present day problems when because of falling congregations the chapel had to close. The chapel next to the police-station was taken over by the local Thespian Society and the other by the Salvation Army after their previous citadel in Station Lane had to be closed due to mining subsidence.

One of the highlights on a Sunday for us Hawson Street kids was when the Salvation Army held an open-air meeting down our street. They had a big membership in those days and a big band. After the meeting we would march behind the band as they made their way back to the Citadel in Station Lane. My time at Wombwell Salvation Army was a defining time in my life where I matured from being a gang member of the Hawson Streeters to accepting God in my life. It was there that I found one could make friends with many other young people and not have to conform to a gang code. It was there I first fell madly and hopelessly in love and then failed miserably to meet the standards required of me, but the experience changed my life and gave me a strong determination to live a good and Christian life.

The National Health Service (NHS)....

The Labour Party was elected to government immediately after the end of WW2. For many its biggest achievement was the formation of the NHS in 1948. It was a vitally urgent service as the nation's health after years of stringent food rationing was very poor. My first tooth extraction was pulled by a school dentist, but other services such as fillings were not given as most school children at that time were suffering from a poor diet throughout the war and just needed to have bad teeth removed.

Three of the early benefits of the NHS and highly valued by the working-class was free medicine on a doctor's prescription; free dentistry and free spectacles. There were few doctors available during the war as most of them had been called to military service, but older doctors serving many patients' would still make regular home visits when needed. Many adults suffered from poor oral hygiene and in most cases all the dentists could do was to extract all their teeth and supply them with a free set of false teeth which they would previously have not been able to afford. At one time it seemed that all adults were being given false teeth and also supplied with free glasses but by 1951 the demand was so great and so costly to the government struggling with an economic crisis that the government had to place a one shilling charge on a doctor's prescription and patients were required to pay half the cost for new dentures and glasses.

Friday (pay day) was the day collectors would call for payments of rent and other services. There was one old chap who would come down the street every Friday on his bicycle even in some of the worst winter weather and he never missed. It was a while before I realised he was collecting payment for past medical services to the family prior to the NHS. Mum never missed a payment and had to continue paying off the debt for several years after the NHS had started.

Chemist shops....

Chemist shops in the Valley were very different from what they are today; they were also the only place where certain products could be bought. Toilet paper wasn't sold in grocery shops and toilet paper that was available due to the demand for paper for the war effort, was sold in loose leaf pads and smelt strongly of Izal – a very strong local disinfectant. Feminine hygiene products were purchased by a whisper over the counter to a female assistant and then passed over the counter in a brown paper bag. I often thought the local birth rate was high due to the fact that chemist shops seemed to employ only young pretty assistants. The problem with that being men were too embarrassed to ask them for condoms and subsequently had to rely on their occasional visit to the barber's shop where after a hair-cut the barber would politely enquire if sir needed anything for the week-end? This must be an indication that in those early years, the working men and women in the Valley only managed to get it together at the week-end.

Education in the Valley....

As a predominantly Valley mining town, my home town of Wombwell was populated mostly by miners' families; however there was no neglect of education even if it was not always the best. It would be true to say that a few of us youngsters in the Valley left school with little more than the basics of education sufficient to see us through the working life for which we were destined. Most young chaps like me went straight to the mines from school. Those like me who were fortunate not to work underground were called-up for National Service when they were eighteen and were often sent overseas within weeks of completing basic training.

My schooling started at the age of three at Park Street nursery school (now demolished). At the age of five I was moved to the primary section and it was there I first came across education segregation. Even in poor mining towns class elitism reared its ugly head. At a very young age it was obvious to me that teachers' children and the children of the Wombwell elite were all seated in a separate area to the left side of the classroom and received more and special attention than the rest of the class. Consequently when the time came to move to the junior school they were far better prepared than we were.

The move to junior school was a traumatic experience as we had been previously warned by older children about horrible teachers and harsh punishments. It was in junior school that our education really started. I did reasonably well but I could never get the hang of maths. I could cope with the basics but anything complicated defeated me. The extra attention for children of the elite was repeated throughout the four years at junior school, consequently the remainder of us didn't get attention when we needed it.

However, I did succeed in being made class monitor for ink and cod-liver oil. Class monitors were responsible for distributing pencils, pen-nibs and blotting paper. Ink monitors had to mix the ink powder with water and top-up the ink wells inserted in the top of desks. This was a messy job and enabled me and my pal to spend at least fifteen minutes out of class scrubbing the ink off our fingers.

All junior school pupils received a quarter pint of milk every day. Each class had two milk monitors who would fetch the crate of milk for their class from where the local co-op milk lorry delivered it outside the main door. We would distribute the milk and later collect the empty bottles and return the crate outside ready for collection the next morning. The upside for milk monitors was that we would collect the quantity of bottles for the full class, but as there was always somebody absent we were able to drink the spare bottles before we returned to class.

'Oil monitor' might seem an unusual job but was very necessary as many children during the war years were seriously malnourished and after examination by a school doctor would be recommended for a daily dose of cod-liver-oil. As the oil monitor I had a register with all their names and how many doses they were to receive. At the morning break I would line the kids up and administer one or two spoonfuls as indicated on the register and then sign to say they had had their dose. My heart bled for those kids especially the little ones who were mostly thin, malnourished and always seemed frightened. It must have been ghastly to swallow the raw oil without anything to take away the horrible taste. Some would make a mad dash for the cloakroom and a drink of water, others sometimes just threw up where they stood. Many would have gone to school with little breakfast to talk of and the impact of the oil on an empty stomach would have been horrible. My instructions were that if they threw-up I had to give them another dose but I could never bring myself to do that. It was always possible to tell who the kids were on the oil register because they seemed to continually smell of fish oil. As a senior at junior school I always made a point of protecting those kids and they knew they could always come to me for help. Meanwhile I could knock off fifteen minutes out of class washing the spoons and scrubbing the smell from my hands.

We did physical exercises every other day either in the playground or the school hall depending on the weather. The highlight of the week for us was the games period every Friday afternoon and the last period of the day: the girls would play 'rounders' while the boys played a game called 'skittle'. I soon realised why it was the last period of the week as skittle was the most brutal game I have ever experienced. Senior boys aged 10 and 11 would be divided into two teams and given a coloured sash for team identification. There were no rules and crying through injury was not allowed. The teacher (referee) would place a small wood skittle at each end of the playground and to start the game he would blow his whistle and throw the ball in the air. The sole objective was to knock down the other team's skittle. This could only happen once as when a skittle had been downed the game was over. After a week in school and the relief of the coming week-end, the lads went at it with fanatical enthusiasm. The scrimmage would roll all over the school playground and often spilled over into the school corridors scattering screaming girls in all directions as the mei-lee just followed the ball wherever it went. Bloody noses, black eyes and bruised limbs, not to mention torn clothing were all carried away proudly after the game.

The attendance of a teacher at the game was solely to prevent serious injuries taking place and to blow the final whistle when a skittle was downed. The much talked about Eton wall game was tame by comparison to the Park Street skittle game. When I read about what children are not allowed to do in playgrounds today, I become very concerned about the future development of boys. Some of the older boys who were with me at junior school went on to serve their country in combat areas with the armed-forces, while some of us younger chaps served National Service and saw military service in many overseas locations. I firmly believe we were well prepared to cope with the adversities of battle should our country have required us to do so. I do not believe I could say the same about many young lads in school today; growing-up in a nanny-state and surrounded by pervasive feminism. When we were injured at school there was never any thought of our parents blaming the school or teachers. We carried our injuries as a badge of honour to be displayed with pride.

Although it was never admitted, students in the final year at junior school and prior to the 11+ exam; were separated by teachers into those who could pass the exam, those who might pass and those who wouldn't pass. This exam determined those who went to grammar school and those who went to secondary modern school. The two sections that could pass were given extensive support by teachers while we that were regarded as unlikely to pass were abandoned. Even at eleven years of age I resented this because I believed I could have stood a chance with extra support with my maths. All my other subjects, in spite of my monitoring duties were above average and in a mock exam prior to the 11+ exam I wrote an essay that the headmaster was so pleased with that he read it to the full school at assembly. It's almost certain I would never have made a rocket scientist but I could have made a mark in other subjects where I was strong such as History and English if I had had the benefit of a grammar school education.

I have always supported the separation of children into grammar, technical and secondary schools and also by examination at the age of eleven. There is no value in giving a quality education to a child that has no real interest in pursuing further education. Many of the lads at my school just wanted to get out of school and earn some money and that attitude still exists today. Sadly, one of my mates who passed the exam lasted only one year and then was sent down to a secondary school. I was annoyed at the waste of his place as I had desperately wanted to go to grammar school. However, the lack of a grammar school or university education did not affect my career in business where I excelled well beyond many of my colleagues who had the benefit of a grammar and university education.

Although a secondary modern education was considered inferior in the school system, we nonetheless had the advantage of some excellent and dedicated teachers who must have found it frustrating that the end product of their efforts were destined to spend their working lives breathing coal dust in a mine until their damaged lungs gave up on them. The four years of secondary education allocated to us before leaving school at fifteen were good years. For many soon to be coal miners, 'the best years of our lives'. Discipline was strict but always fair. We enjoyed a lot of good sport and even some cultural activities such as school plays, choirs and even an occasional visit from an orchestra.

Being somewhat challenged in height has always been a handicap to me but I always stood my ground whether at school, in the army, in business or in politics. My hard attitude must have come to the attention of my teachers and headmaster for when I reached standard four (the last year of school) and the names of new prefects were announced by the headmaster at assembly I found that I had been appointed head prefect.

My father was very proud and promised to help me with a problem my appointment was going to cause me. Boys at the school had always worn short trousers but over the previous two years long trousers had started to appear (mostly worn by children from better-off families) and with second and first year boys wearing long trousers. All the other prefects also wore long trousers and I believed I would be open to ridicule if I continued to wear short trousers. Being height challenged I knew I was going to have a tough time in any event with cocky youngsters; wearing short trousers would have made the problem worse. I had to plead with my parents that I couldn't possibly be head prefect if I was open to ridicule if I continued to wear short trousers. Dad was sympathetic but he was reluctant to interfere with Mum's clothing plans and with the new term starting in September the next clothing purchase was only scheduled for May. Eventually some of my older siblings persuaded Mum that in view of my new status and the pride of the family (I was first on the male side to be head prefect although others had been prefects) I should have some long trousers. Mum gave in but only on condition they were my Christmas present. With a huge sigh of relief I agreed.

Being made head prefect and having long trousers did wonders for my love life. I suppose girls just like many women are attracted to power and status as I found out when numerous invitations to parties and walks in the park began to arrive. It says something of the way relationships have changed since I was at school in 1949, when I had to turn down one girl who I really fancied because she was only in standard two and two years younger than me which would have exposed me to being accused of 'cradle snatching'. But fate was on my side as when I was on army leave from Gibraltar and she was a nursing student at Mexborough Technical College, we met by chance on Wombwell High Street and were able to spend a very enjoyable leave together.

Leaving school for me was very traumatic. Although I was excited at the prospect of earning a wage and having pocket money, I found leaving school to be almost like leaving home. Life had been good to me at school and I had a good idea of the sordid working conditions waiting for me at the mine.

Houghton Main Colliery....

Houghton Main Colliery was one of the largest and most productive coal-mines in the Valley and where my Dad and older brothers had been employed for many years. Employment at Houghton Main was not automatic for all applicants but preference was always given to those like me who had relatives employed at the mine and my Dad being foreman boiler-fireman also helped. Dad seemed to be very proud when he took me to sign on at the colliery offices. I was accepted on a training course that involved three months training at an old disused mine at Brierley where we were taught basic underground skills and also at Hemsworth technical college where we were taught essential technical requirements.

However, my underground mining career was brought to an abrupt end. In 1946 the Labour government under Prime Minister Clement Atlee nationalised the coal mines and created the National Coal Board (NCB) who had immediately instituted compulsory training schemes before any employee was allowed to work underground and also introduced a strict medical and fitness examination. It came as a bombshell to me when I was taken off the course after failing the medical examination. I was told that I was not yet tall enough to meet the requirements for underground work. Although it was a relief in many respects it was also a severe dent to my pride as most of my school mates passed their medical. I had always been able to cope with my lack of height but the doctors were not prepared to make any allowances.

I had to accept the situation and was given a job on the pit-top screens and the day I had to report there was one of the worst of my life. Firstly, I had to change into working clothes in the colliery baths that was full of miners either showering after their shift or changing into working clothes. The appearance of this little guy attracted some attention, but no scorn. Miners by their nature are friendly and considerate and I soon had plenty of helpers to show me the ropes. Two of them who were due to go down the mine walked me up to the screens (where I was to work) and handed me over to the foreman. I would never have found my way without them and we later became good friends. After the first day the baths ordeal gradually got better. The miners would banter with me but were never hurtful and although I knew few of their names they all seemed to know mine.

Entering the pit-head baths for the first time was an experience never to be forgotten. Over three hundred miners would be using the baths every day. I was hit with the horrible, nauseous smell of dirty, sweaty bodies, clothes and steam. It was a smell I never got used to and was there every time I entered the baths. I do not in any way denigrate the men who used those baths as I also used them. Their objective was only to wash away the dirt and sweat so they could go home clean to their families. I must also emphasise that the baths were always kept in an excellent condition by a dedicated baths staff.

Although the pit-baths had terrified me initially, I later became very appreciative for the facility even after I had moved out of dirty jobs. As a youngster my bathing consisted of one bath a week being scrubbed by my Mum in a bath in front of the fire, but as I grew older she would give me sixpence to pay for a 'slipper bath' at the local swimming baths once a week. I never discovered why they were called 'slipper baths', but one section of the local swimming baths contained about ten cabins with baths and catered for those like myself who did not have bathing facilities at home. Lady attendants would fill the baths from taps located on the outside and would check the temperature of the water to make sure it wasn't too hot. I disliked this weekly ritual because I was embarrassed with a lady running me a bath and also having to sit in a queue waiting for a bath to become vacant. After being appointed to the Landsale Office I still took advantage of being able to use the pit-head baths to take a shower every working day. Although I didn't use the baths when shifts were changing at 5am and 2pm every day, I still occasionally bumped into some of the men who I met on the first few days of my induction to the pit-head baths. They would stop and have a chat with me and were very impressed with my progress in the short time I had been at the mine and would chaff me about being 'staff or management'.

I often look back on those days with great nostalgia. Coal miners were truly the salt of the earth and I considered myself very privileged to have been accepted by them. I was deeply concerned in later years that they may have felt I had betrayed them politically, when at many elections I was an anti-Labour candidate when nearly all miners were solidly Labour. On several occasions some people I knew accused me of betraying my roots, even some of my own family. But my old friends from Houghton Main colliery would still acknowledge me and give me a cheery wave if we met at a polling-station, in spite of the presence of Labour Party officials. As one old pal told me, "They don't know where the cross goes on the ballot-paper", and quite a few must have voted for me as I never lost a local election.

Working on the screens where I was initially assigned was truly a job from hell. It involved standing at the side of a conveyor belt for eight hours a-day hand sorting dross from coal. Tubs of coal would be brought to the surface and put onto a rail system where they would run downhill from the pit-head and then be stopped by a guy with a wooden instrument called a 'chokker' at a check-weigh. Inside the check-weigh were two weigh-men whose job it was to record and agree the weight of the coal coming from a seam marked by chalk on the side of the tub. One of the men represented the NCB management, and the other the miners' union. After the weigh-in the tubs ran down a small incline to a tipper that turned the tubs upside down and emptied the coal on to a conveyor belt underneath where the contents were screened and any dross inside removed.

As the tubs were turned over on the conveyor belt approximately two every minute, there were constant clouds of coal dust. When being placed at the belt by the foreman for the first time (this was a job that required zero training) I recoiled in horror, when through the clouds of coal dust I could see only the eyes of people on the other side of the belt. I stood there on that first day and to my shame I cried, the tears creating rivulets through coal dust accumulating on my cheeks. Here I was, a lad of fifteen asking myself if this was what

I went to school for; a lad who had been head prefect and now reduced to working at a belt with zombies.

The workers on the screen belts were mostly old and disabled men who had been transferred to surface work after becoming unfit to work underground. After my first shift I told my Dad what it was like and that I would stick it out for the time being but there was no way I was going to stay in that job. Eventually I got to know the men I was working with and later I was invited to join them in the snap cabin (snap is sandwiches – in a tin). We took food to work in a snap tin and usually a bottle of cold tea with no milk. There were no thermos flasks at the time, and at first I thought drinking tea that way was revolting but eventually thirst got the better of me and I would finish the bottle by the end of the shift.

Although snap time was short (20 minutes) I was amazed at the depth of discussion that took place. The cabin was just big enough for about thirty men sitting on planks around the perimeter. Talk would usually start with horse racing, graduate to the Labour Party and government and then complaints about working conditions. Eventually I started taking part in the discussions and I must admit that I felt a bit superior being just out of school and quite knowledgeable about politics for my age. Horse racing though was the main topic and because of my small height I was constantly urged by the men to apply to be an apprentice jockey. The possibility certainly appealed to me and one of the men obtained details for me to apply to one of the top stables. When I received a reply inviting me to an interview I was really thrilled, but my Dad would have none of it and made it very clear I was to go no further with my application. Dad was not a gambling man and was very critical of working men on low wages wasting their money on horse-racing. So although I was desperate to get away from the mine and live and work in the fresh air and the countryside, it was not to be as I had to respect Dad's wishes.

Shortly after a train of events changed my working life at the mine and after reflection I realised that it was due partly to the respect in which my Dad as foreman boiler-fireman was held at the mine by pit-top management. I was thrilled to get away from the screens when the foreman asked me to take a job as a 'dabber'. Dabbing involved holding a thick piece of rope and splayed at the end which had to be dipped into a tub of water and used to wash off the coal face numbers on the coal tubs after they had passed over the check-weigh and before they were returned underground. The job was tedious and monotonous and bitterly cold in winter as the process took place in the open area between the check-weigh and the tipper. But I had no complaints as anything was better than standing at a conveyor belt breathing in clouds of coal dust hour after hour.

I must have done a good job because shortly after I was called to the office of the pit-top manager who was with the chief colliery engineer and asked if I would like to work in the engine-room. As the job was a regular day-shift job I accepted straight away as I hated having to work alternate weeks on the afternoon and evening shift. However, when I was first taken to the winding-room I was horrified and thought I had made a big mistake. It was the first time I'd seen the huge engine with its massive pistons thrashing up and down. This was the engine that powered two cages up and down the pit shaft lifting men and coal to the surface or dropping men and empty tubs to the pit bottom. My job was to keep the engine-room spotlessly clean and all the many pieces of the engine well oiled. The most dangerous part was having to climb into the piston-well where the giant pistons rested when the engine stopped to remove any grease or dirt that may have accumulated on the piston heads. When I saw the piston required attention and before going into the well I had to shout to the engine-winder 'going in'. The engine driver (winder) sat on a big raised platform with the driving gear and was out of sight where I had to go into the piston well. I then had to wait for a clear response from him before going into the well (my life was in his hands) then when I had finished I would shout 'going out' signalling to him that it was safe to restart winding.

This was one job where training was most certainly needed but once I overcame the initial fear I settled into the job and enjoyed what I had to do. Every morning around 8am the chief engineer would inspect the engine-room and speak to the winder on duty. He was always pleased with my work and I believe it was his recommendation that after about six months in the winding-room, he told me I had to report to a Mr Harold Smith at the Landsale Office to be interviewed for a position in his office. I couldn't believe my luck when I got the job, especially as I would be working office hours and I no longer had to be out of bed at 4.30am to catch a bus at 5am to get to the colliery and start work at 6am.

This was a truly momentous phase in my life. Mr Smith referred to as 'Smithy' behind his back, became my mentor as well as my boss. He was very patient with me and helped me to quickly settle-in to my new responsibilities. There was a constant stream of senior management through our office including most of the under-managers who would call at the office for a last smoke before going underground. They would engage Smithy in conversation and listening-in I very quickly became knowledgeable about the management of the mine.

Politics often came up for discussion by various managers, overmen and other mine officials visiting the office. A regular visitor was George Wilkinson, secretary of the Houghton Main branch of the National Union of Mineworkers. George was a communist while Smithy was a die-hard Tory who bitterly resented the nationalisation of the coal industry. They had some fearsome arguments to which I would listen with great interest. Another frequent visitor was George Fearons the mine training officer who during WWI had received a battlefield commission and entranced me with details of the many battles. George loaned me several books on the Liberal Party and wet my appetite further for politics. Another official I became friends with was Arthur Gledhill who was the colliery safety officer who had also gained a battlefield commission in WWI. What is probably not well known or documented is that many men from the Valley distinguished themselves in battle and were promoted to the commissioned ranks.

Part of my job was to issue the pit-top men with their pay slips on a Thursday which they would then present to the pay-office on a Friday for their wages. It had never occurred to me the level of status attached to being selected to work in the Landsale Office, but the men knew and showed their respect. They would queue at an office window, state their name and as I handed them their pay slip they would touch their cap and say thank you sir, even though I was only a sixteen year-old boy who not long ago had been sharing a snap cabin with some of them. The first time my Dad came to the window to collect his pay slip, he touched his cap just like the other men and I could hardly hold my tears back. As I turned from the window I noticed Smithy was watching and in a gentle voice he said, 'It's just habit Peter'. When I saw Dad at home later I told him he must never touch his cap to me again. He just looked at me and said, 'OK son'. I knew that he was very proud that his son had made it to the Landsale Office.

I matured very fast in the two years I worked with Smithy and prior to being called-up for National Service. Additionally I had the advantage of exposure to educated and knowledgeable people that developed my understanding of work related and political issues way beyond my years. As a junior I was often required to run errands for senior management and most days I would receive a telephone call from the colliery manager to collect his cigarettes from the colliery canteen. Being the bearer of his cigarettes I was authorised to bypass the queue outside his office and enter without knocking which seemed to impress those waiting to see him and enabled me to falsely assume a status way beyond my position. I mentioned this to dad and he told me had been employed at the mine for over forty years and mostly as foreman boiler-man of the team that stoked the huge boilers that provided the steam to drive the huge engines that kept the mine in operation, but he had never met any of the mine managers and had never seen the inside of the manager's office. Although these were the days of nationalisation and a new era in the coal-mining industry, the old culture of the master and servant was still there and it was a long time before it disappeared.

I was surprised to learn when Dad eventually reached compulsory retiring age and had to leave his job, that there was no farewell or thank you very much for your long service and here is a gold watch or something similar to mark an employee's dedicated service. These old chaps on retiring just emptied their locker in the pit-head baths, handed in their keys and collected their last pay packet.

National Service....

It is a fact that historically most men in the Valley had always been involved in the coal-mining industry which was a big priority for Britain's industry, but they were still always called to meet the nation's military needs. And so it was that with the introduction of National Service (NS), underground workers were exempt from NS but those employed in the many essential jobs on the surface were still required for call-up.

Most of the famous Yorkshire infantry regiments such as the East Yorks, the West Yorks and the York and Lancs who had fought valiantly in many of Britain's many battles, had long since been disbanded due to cuts in defence spending, while most of the more prestigious regiments in the south were spared. The only artillery regiment in the Valley at the time was the 271 Sheffield Field Regiment, which was only a Territorial Army (TA) regiment. Subsequently all the lads from the Valley called to serve NS in the army were allocated to artillery regiments so that when they completed NS they could be allocated to a local TA to serve their compulsory three years on the reserve. This didn't go down very well with the lads as the artillery regiments appeared to be lacking in any sort of 'Flashman' like glamour. So it was much to my surprise that while all my mates had been allocated to the Royal Artillery, when my papers arrived I was instructed to report to the 1st.Bn The Duke of Wellington's infantry regiment at Wellesley Barracks, Halifax, a prestigious West Yorkshire infantry regiment.

Prior to receiving my call-up papers I had to report to the medical examination centre in Doncaster. It was there I had been previously examined and medically rejected for underground work. I was terrified I would once again be rejected as being too small and would have to face the humiliation of seeing my mates going off to the army without me. However, much to my surprise and relief I was passed fit AI. There must still be many former army NS men living in the Valley and for most of us NS was an experience never to be forgotten. I have never met any former NS men who would not claim it to be one of the most defining times of their life.

On the 12th February 1953, my parents waved goodbye to me as I walked up Hawson Street with my suitcase to catch a Burrow's bus to Barnsley and then a Yorkshire Traction bus to Huddersfield and then another bus to Halifax where I was to report to the Regimental Depot before 12 noon. It was bitterly cold and snowing heavily as I joined the lads who I was to spend the next two years with and the fierce looking drill instructors who were to be our tormentors for the next eight weeks. Most of my new mates were local lads who had been employed in the industries and mills around Halifax, Huddersfield and Bradford, with a sprinkling of farm lads from the Pennine farms. I was soon identified as a foreigner even though my home town of Wombwell wasn't all that far away. But the joshing I got was all friendly and I was soon accepted in the same way as the farm lads who were often the butt of many jokes. During the torture of basic training we soon came together as a team and many long time friendships were formed.

The first day was mostly spent drawing kit from the various stores and making energy sapping journeys laden with equipment across the parade ground already deep in snow. Next we were marched to the medical centre for another medical and a series of vaccinations before collecting eating utensils and joining the queue at the cookhouse. Whether it was the freezing cold outside and the hot atmosphere in the cookhouse or the effect of the vaccinations, I don't know, but as we stood in the queue for the servery chaps started dropping to the ground in a faint with their crockery smashing and creating almost pandemonium. I finally got to the servery and had some food sloshed on to my plate and then found a seat. As I sat trying to eat the food I contemplated what lay ahead, all of a sudden two years and my Valley seemed a long time away.

I'm not going to relate all the day to day details of our basic training accept to say we were treated as men (although we were little more than boys) and expected to behave like men. The hours were long and the discipline harsh. I sometimes dragged my aching body into bed at night and prayed I wouldn't wake-up in the morning. But the end result after eight weeks was that we could march and do complicated drills on foot and with a rifle. We knew every single piece of our weapons so well we could strip them down and put them back together in the dark. We could assemble and throw hand-grenades and scream with intent as we made bayonet charges; we could silently attack enemy positions and respond immediately to commands. In short we were transformed into credible soldiers and it was even possible to see the respect on our instructors faces.

The salute at our passing-out parade was taken by the Mayor of Halifax. The previous night we had prepared our uniforms to perfection so that when the CO inspected us before the parade he congratulated us on an excellent turnout, and he also congratulated our instructors, who in all fairness had had a tough job turning raw young boys into fighting men. After the parade and photographs taken with our officers and instructors we were sent on a two-week embarkation leave. We should have been joining the 1st Battalion in Korea, but the armistice was signed just before we finished basic training, instead we were told to expect a transfer to the Gordon Highlanders who were fighting the Ma Mau insurgency in Kenya. After a very enjoyable leave and on returning to the depot, much to my delight we were sent on another two weeks leave as our departure had not been finalised.

Eventually we were told we would be joining the Dukes 1st Battalion who had left Korea and were now in Gibraltar. Arriving in Gibraltar we had to do another six weeks advance training that was also tough but was easier to cope with after our training at the regimental depot. Gibraltar in 1953 was not the holiday and tourist destination it is today. Conditions were very basic and due to a shortage of water and limited catchment facilities, we were restricted to one pint of drinking water a day. Bathing had to be in salt water for which we were supplied with a special soap supposedly to make a lather, but it didn't really work so all the body hair had to come off. Because the Rock always faced the possibility of a siege by Franco's Spain, masses of food had to be stored in huge storage facilities inside the Rock. Consequently all new food supplies went in on one side of the rock and the oldest came out the other side and found its way to the many military cookhouses. Meals were incredibly bad and my mates and me seemed to survive on chip banjos (chip sandwiches always in big demand at the NAAFI) then on pay day there would be a rush to Smokey Joe's cafe just outside the barracks where we could binge on platefuls of chips, eggs and baked beans with two slices of bread to soak up the grease.

Duties mostly consisted of guard duties at the frontier with Spain, the Governor's official residence known as The Convent and ceremonial duties for visiting royalty and VIP's. Training however never stopped and we were in a constant state of preparedness. Much to our disappointment we never got the chance to see action, except that on one occasion we were put on alert to go to some place in North Africa where local tribesman were threatening trouble. After spending two days on the airport tarmac with all our equipment we were eventually stood down. Although there is always a lot of sympathy for young men being sent in to action, I would guess that that at least 90% of NS men in infantry regiments were desperate to see action. When the ceasefire was agreed in Korea just before we finished basic training we were extremely disappointed that action finished before we got there.

The battalion received orders to return to the UK in January 1955 and I was lucky to be selected for the advance party that arrived in England in December 1954.

After being on my hobby-horse about the benefits of NS, I've often been asked, 'Well what did it do for you'? In fact it taught us young, immature adolescents to endure, to obey, self-reliance, team work and to make our minds and bodies cope with adversity. It taught us self-pride, respect for others and that after service there was the reward of returning to a free society, a society that can only be sustained and appreciated through service. I can honestly say that I'm deeply grateful to the officers and non-commissioned officers who put me through the mill and turned me from a boy into a man and made me fit to go out into the world with confidence and self-discipline. I have often said and still believe that young men and women of today would benefit substantially from doing National Service.

One of my proudest possessions is my National Service medal.

Return to the Valley....

My Valley had always been a dark Valley full of back-to-back houses and crowded streets. Although it was home and deeply loved, everything and everybody seemed consumed in coal-dust, soot and grime. As youngsters we enjoyed many games in the streets but often had to stop to let funerals pass of which there always seemed to be many. Most of the dead were old men dying from lung disease after a lifetime in the mines, but even the young weren't spared with many dying from tuberculosis, pneumonia and scarlet fever. I was sixteen before I went on my first family holiday to Rhyll in North Wales for a full week. I was so overwhelmed with the sheer beauty and seeing large ships passing by that I convinced myself that I should runaway and get a job on a ship just like my Dad when he joined the Merchant Navy. It never happened, but the seed was planted and I knew that one day I had to escape from my Valley that seemed to be continually shrouded in a suffocating darkness.

Although I never got a chance to sail the seas like Dad, national service gave me the opportunity I needed. After two years in the army and experiencing the wonders of life outside the Valley, I knew that my return to the colliery would have to be brief. It was good to be back home among family and friends but each day back at the mine was more than I could stand, and although I had been given a good clerical job, after three months I just walked out irrespective of the consequences. I was unemployed for nearly six months apart from a one month job I got as a labourer with a local builder. The little savings I had were soon gone and I was totally broke. My Mum God bless her would buy me a packet of Park Drive cigarettes every Friday even though she couldn't really afford it. I wasn't prepared to continue sponging on Mum and Dad so one day I told Dad that I had decided to rejoin the army and asked him if he would loan me the money to travel to the Dukes regimental depot at Halifax to join the regular army. He was wasn't too happy about me going back to the army and suggested I should give it a while longer. I had been making lots of job applications but with no education certificates behind me I wasn't getting anywhere. One day in sheer desperation I had written an application for a vacancy for a trainee manager stating that I had three 'O' levels, which I wasn't too concerned about because I didn't expect a reply.

To satisfy Mum and Dad I waited for another two weeks but no job came my way and I firmly believed I had no alternative but to join the army, so once again I had to ask Dad for a loan to travel to Halifax. My parents were not happy about my decision but finally agreed. The next morning Mum made me a magnificent breakfast almost as though it was going to be my last meal. I packed my suitcase and was almost on the point of saying goodbye when there was a knock on the front door. Dad went to the door and there was a young woman there from Lipton's the retail store with whom I had applied for a job and who I had also said untruthfully that I had three 'O' levels. She gave Dad a note inviting me to attend an interview the next day. Dad was thrilled and said I should at least wait another day and give the interview a chance.

Although I didn't fancy my chances at the interview I felt I had to go to satisfy Mum and Dad. The next day I set off for the interview with a great deal of trepidation and wondering what excuses I could make for not bringing my 'O' level certificates with me. Miraculously I wasn't asked and to my total surprise I was offered a job. I went home on cloud nine but at the back of my mind was the thought they would ask for my certificates later but they didn't. I often think back how that young woman from Lipton's caught me almost within minutes of losing out on a highly successful business career. June Deakin worked alongside me for several years as I moved up the management ladder and she later came to work for me in one of my business enterprises. She will always occupy a special place in my life.

Lipton Limited....

Sir Thomas Lipton was known throughout the Valley as the rich merchant who had gained a worldwide reputation for his successes in international sailing competitions, but Sir Thomas was also the owner of one of Britain's biggest grocery and provisions chains. After his death his reputation for the standards of retailing and service to the public continued. By the time I joined Lipton's it was part of a huge group that controlled other popular retail groups such as the Home and Colonial, the Meadow Dairy and the Maypole. Most of these shops were represented in towns throughout the Valley and although part of the same group and supplied from the same warehouses, they were still fiercely competitive.

I was somewhat fortunate to join the company in 1955 when the concept of self-service was starting to take-off. Previously the shops were all counter-service with shop assistants struggling to cope with hordes of women standing at the counters waiting to be served and often falling-out over was next in turn to be served. It was an incredibly frustrating process for customers and assistants as some customers could take a long time to go through their shopping list.

I was allocated to the local Lipton's in Barnsley for my initial training. Fortuitously this store had been selected by the company to develop its self-service business, so I was able to take advantage of being one of the first young managers to be trained in self-service operations. But firstly I had to be trained in all the basic shop skills with the preparation of provisions being high on the agenda. This involved deboning sides of bacon and preparing the various cuts for presentation in the shop window. I had to quickly learn how to prepare a large range of cooked meats and cheeses and the methods of display as well as attending to strict hygiene and cleaning processes. My first introduction to serving on a counter was a nightmare particularly as the young female counter assistants took advantage of my nervousness, but it was something that could only be overcome with time and eventually I was able to cope and eventually even take control of a busy counter.

Joining Lipton's did wonders for my social life. The shops were mostly staffed by young women most of whom had joined the company straight from school. They were exceptionally quick on the counters and were a brash perky lot who delighted in embarrassing young apprentices carrying trays of products to the counters. One young chubby apprentice had his belt removed and his trousers pulled down while both his hands were trying to cope with a big tray of bacon. Fortunately apprentices wore long aprons and as he struggled to protect his dignity the customers were unaware what was taking place. There was a constant turnover of female assistants as they did not often stay past the age of twenty as they were in big demand for marriage; they were also considered to have been left on the shelf if they had not married by the time they were twenty-one. Consequently we trainees always looked forward to a new intake of bright young females once every year.

Although I was being trained specifically in self-service, as I progressed I was often sent out to manage counter-shops when managers went on leave or were taken ill. This was another nightmare at first because I had little knowledge of counter only shops, but it gave me the opportunity to exercise my management skills in which I must have been successful because after three years I was appointed manager of the self-service branch at Barnsley. This caused a lot of resentment from much older managers who had a history of employment with the company. The Barnsley branch being the first company self-service store was considered a plum appointment and most of the managers believed it to be totally illogical for a young twenty four year-old man to be given so much responsibility.

Although the previous manager had the distinction of being the company's first self-service store manager his heart was not in self-service and he yearned for the days he spent in counter-service shops. When the opportunity came along for him to take a position as area manager in charge of counter-service shops he jumped at the chance. I couldn't believe my luck at being given such an opportunity and took-up the challenge with great enthusiasm. Within two years I tripled the store's takings and was soon acknowledged as one of the company's top managers. The confidence in me by the company's management must have been high as a decision was taken to build the company's biggest supermarket in Barnsley and I was appointed to open and manage the store.

The opening of the biggest supermarket in the Valley was a big and exciting event. Opening day saw huge queues winding around all the town-centre streets and blocking the pavements, resulting in police having to assist with crowd control. At times I had to order the closure of the store's doors every fifteen minutes to enable staff to cope with the huge volume of customers. Although it is quite ordinary in retail stores today, in 1963 a store in the Valley selling a large range of grocery products with a large deli and provision counters, butchery, fruit and vegetables and a large non-food department all under one roof was an exciting experience for shoppers and was hugely successful.

Prior to the store opening I had spent time training in areas where I had no previous experience such as deli, butchery, and non-foods. With professional training I soon gained enough experience and confidence to be able to recruit a management team capable of managing large turnovers, and in the process incurring further wrath from some company managers who had expected to make a move into supermarkets but whose long counter-shop experience I felt did not make them suitable for supermarket retailing. The only concern I had right up to opening day was with the deli. Customers in Barnsley had not previously seen or had the exposure to a vast range of continental products. On the opening morning and prior to the doors opening I expressed my concern to the deli manager that the pile of French brie in round containers would still be there at the end of the day. I was wrong as by the end of the day the deli counter was almost stripped clean and we had to organise replenishment stocks overnight to be ready for the rush the following day. In reality, I believe it could be said that in opening the town's first supermarket we transformed the shopping and eating habits of the citizens of the Valley and made meal times far more appetising than the basic range of products on which they had existed for many years.

The Barnsley supermarket was a tremendous success for the company and also for my future ambitions, as after just one year I was promoted to operations executive controlling the company's supermarkets in the north of England. As the spread of supermarkets continued to grow, I have to confess I was saddened to see the destruction of so many small family owned shops that had provided decades of quality service to local communities. One casualty in the Valley was the Barnsley British Co-operative Society (BBCS) whose shops and stores had supported local communities through many dark times, but the BBCS mostly managed by local Labour Party politicians and supporters failed to react to the changes taking place in retailing and lost the battle to continue serving the public they had served so loyally for many years.

Politics...and Wombwell Urban District Council....

How I found time to get involved in politics and local government still amazes me, but my enthusiasm started in 1945 when at the age of ten and still in junior school I became involved in my first general-election. Throughout the war years I was a fanatical supporter of Winston Churchill my war-time hero and although my family and the Valley were solidly Labour I felt compelled to offer my assistance to the Conservative Party fighting the Dearne Valley constituency election from their base in Wombwell.

One day a scruffy young lad in short trousers walked into the Conservative constituency office in Church Street, Wombwell and asked if he could help. Two very well dressed and superior looking men looked at me in astonishment, then after recovering one of them pointed to large piles of what looked like newspapers but were the Party's election manifesto. He said I should deliver as many of those as I possibly could to all the houses in Wombwell. Every day for seven days before the election I faithfully reported to the office and collected large bundles of the newspapers and delivered them to as many houses as I could, sometimes working until late at night and all day Saturday and Sunday. I came to the conclusion that there was only me fighting the election because I never so anybody else at the office or involved anywhere else in Wombwell.

The day after the election I stood among a crowd at the bottom of Church Street and opposite Wombwell Town Hall waiting for the announcement of the election result. Eventually the Returning Officer and the candidates appeared on the Town Hall balcony and after the result was announced with a massive majority for Labour the two candidates made speeches. Wilfred Paling made a victory speech. He was later appointed Postmaster General in Clement Atlee's government. During a heated debate in the House of Commons, Paling accused Winston Churchill of being a "dirty Tory dog", to which Churchill replied, "The Rt.Hon member for Dearne Valley should beware what dogs do to Palings". The Tory candidate Lady Dower, who I had not seen until her appearance on the balcony, in a gesture of defiance said, "I couldn't care less about Dearne Valley so long as we have a Conservative government".

Feeling deflated at the defeat of Churchill's candidate I made my way back to the office and found the same two chaps there who I had met previously. One of them said they were leaving shortly and the room had to be cleared in four days time and could I help them by taking all the unused paper to the council bins. There were still piles of unused newspapers so I readily agreed and said I would also notify the shop downstairs when the room was empty. Quick as a flash I realised the opportunity and set off to canvass all the local fish and chip shops where I negotiated piles of newspapers for bags of chips. I lived on bags of chips for over a week which for a poor lad like me was absolute luxury.

Watching the events taking place on the Town Hall balcony and listening to the cheering crowd was so exciting that I decided there and then that one day I would make a speech from that balcony. In the event it took another nineteen years, but I made it, and with my Mum and Dad watching, it was one of the proudest days of my life.

All fourteen councillors on Wombwell Urban District Council were members of the Labour Party and when I decided to stand in 1964 there hadn't be an election since 1945 as all the Labour ward nominees were returned every year unopposed. It was this fact that drove me to decide this had to stop. Although I was very busy with my career in retailing, I decided to stand as an independent candidate believing that many of the younger generation would not necessarily be steeped in the strong Labour tradition in the Valley. Being raw to electioneering I misread some of the rules for submitting nomination papers, and subsequently submitted my nomination papers with the nominees signatures with the surname first. I had decided to keep my nomination a secret until the last minute, so that when I walked into the Town Clerk's office at one minute before nominations closed as 12 noon my surprise was complete. Unfortunately there was a question as to whether the signatures on my nomination paper would be valid. Consultations took place and eventually the Town Clerk had to consult higher authority at the West Riding County Council. After about fifteen minutes the instruction came back that my nomination papers were valid.

I resided in the South West ward which was by far the largest ward and I was to be up against the Labour Party's chairman of finance. When the Town Clerk posted the nomination papers on the

Town Hall window, Wombwell discovered to great surprise that there was to be a local election which stimulated a great deal of interest. The local press did me proud with a great deal of praise for giving local residents the opportunity to use their vote. I took to campaigning in much the same aggressive way I applied in boosting my company's supermarkets. One of my employees who had just won a beauty competition was roped-in by the press to pose with me.

The council chamber was packed for the count, mostly with Labour Party supporters, my few supporters and the press. When the result was announced by the Town Clerk I had beaten the chairman of finance with a majority of 200 votes which was a substantial margin. At first there was a deadly silence as the Labour Party supporters were stunned with the result. Then my little band of supporters realised what had happened and broke into a cheer. The press could hardly believe what had happened and the local papers were full of my victory for weeks after.

After the first council meeting there was a small social event with beer and sandwiches. Harry Wilkinson, one of the Labour Party's long serving councillors took me on one side and congratulated me on my election. He said I had done well against tremendous odds but he wanted to give me a bit of advice. He said 'Na listen-up lad. If tha iver catches a weasel asleep p..s in its ear. Tha has to understand thes a lot ere toneet who will be trying to p..s in thy ear so be on thi guard at all times. Although we were on opposite sides and often clashed in council debates, Harry remained a valued friend throughout the time we served on the council.

All the Wombwell Labour councillors were miners and the only remuneration they received was to be able to claim for loss of earnings if they had to miss a shift at the mine to attend council and committee meetings. A far cry from the lavish allowances paid to councillors today whether or not they attend meetings.

Although Wombwell was never anything else other than solidly Labour, there must have been many who were pleased to see a local lad who grew-up in Hawson Street, worked at a local mine, went on to be successful in business and then serving as one of their councillors. They must have had a special place for me because in spite of heavy Labour opposition at local elections I was never defeated and continued to serve up to the re-organisation of local government by Edward Heath when Urban District Councils were disbanded, an act of local democratic vandalism by a man who had no knowledge of the value of local government. I decided to join the Liberal Party and in 1978 I was successful in winning a seat to represent Wombwell on the Barnsley Metropolitan District Council. I was the Liberal Party candidate for Dearne Valley at three general-elections during the turbulent 1970's and was able to increase the Liberal vote at each election. Although the Dearne Valley was solidly Labour there were still many among the older miners who could recall the days when the Liberals were the main Party and who had done a great deal to support the miners through some difficult times.

The 1972 miners' strike.........and the rise of Arthur Scargill....

The 1970's were a brutal time for the Valley and particularly for the populations living in coal mining areas. The country was still suffering badly from the incompetence of Harold Wilson's and James Callaghan's Labour governments and by an equally incompetent Edward Heath's Conservative government. It would be true to say that the nation was in turmoil. The introduction of comprehensive schools and the run-down of grammar schools, local government reorganisation and the destruction of grassroots democracy by Edward Heath, all had a pervasive effect on the moral of families who saw their children's future being seriously threatened by the changes taking place. Inflation was rampant and shortages of basic resources were causing many problems for those living on low wages. It was in these circumstances that the miners in the main coal mining areas reached the point where they had had enough and with the support of the majority of NUM members in the Valley decided on the first national coal miners' strike since the devastating miners' strike of 1926, with over 280 000 miners demanding an increase of at least £9 a-week to give them a take-home pay of £25 a-week.

To bridge the gap between ever increasing inflation and their low wages the miners had demanded a 43% wage increase, but the National Coal Board (NCB) offered them only 8%. This was immediately rejected by the miners and it indicated to them that the government had no intention of achieving a realistic solution to the pressing needs of the miners and their families. So the die was cast and with no alternative in sight, on the 9th January 1972 the miners went on strike knowing that once again they faced a long and bitter struggle.

The strike was a huge challenge and opportunity for Arthur Scargill, the rising star in the Yorkshire Miners' Union who had a gift for oratory and leadership skills that helped him organise the miners into an effective force in picketing power stations, coal depots, steelworks and ports. His squadrons of flying picket's successfully closed down the flow of coal with such a devastating effect that on the 9th February the government had to declare a state of emergency and two days later had to introduce a three day working week. Industry had to lay-off thousands of workers and many schools had to close. Fearing that the miners would continue to hold the country to ransom with further unacceptable demands, Edward Heath called a general-election asking the public, "Who rules Britain, the government or the unions?", believing the electorate would support the government. But Heath gambled and lost with the Tories losing control of government by only a slight margin.

Harold Wilson was back in Downing Street and immediately settled the miners' strike with a massive 34% wage increase that propelled the miners back to the top of the best paid workers league.

Peace in the Valley....but not for long....

Relative peace returned to the Valley and other mining areas and the future of the mining industry seemed to be secure to the extent that plans were made for British Coal to produce over 200 million tons of coal by 2000 with further expansion and investment in the industry. But unexpectedly the economy started to change and became less reliant on coal. The government found it became cheaper to import coal from overseas when compared with the ever increasing cost of producing British coal. Eventually the NCB was faced with many loss making pits and was forced to start a pit closure programme.

After the success of the 1972 strike, Arthur Scargill's popularity among the miners surged although he became a hate figure among the general public who feared his extreme left-wing involvement. The announcement of the pit closures and particularly the closure of Cortonwood colliery in the Valley, on Scargill's doorstep, brought a violent reaction from the Yorkshire miners who demanded immediate action to stop the closures.

The strike has been described as one of the most defining events in the history of British industrial relations and is also one of the most defining events in the history of the Valley. One could easily be tempted to look back at our history; all the wars, the terrible pit explosions, unemployment, social misery, the many strikes and all the suffering over the years, and then conclude that this is where it all started to change and change the Valley forever.

The seeds for the 1984/85 miners' strike were sown in the strikes of 1972 and 1974. During those strikes Arthur Scargill demonstrated his leadership strengths and gained a reputation for his tactical ability in getting striking miners and flying picket's to the right places and at the right time. There can be no doubt that it was Scargill's leadership of the miners that brought down Edward Heath's Tory government and later forced Prime Minister Harold Wilson into agreeing two massive wage increases, but even then Scargill was not appeased and immediately slapped in a further claim for a 60% increase.

Years of industrial unrest had brought the Tory government and the nation to an almost economic meltdown. Inflation was out of control and has prices increased alarmingly, so did the unions' demands for further wage increases. It was a 'no-win' situation for both the government and the unions. Although Harold Wilson never admitted the reason for his sudden resignation; all the evidence points to the conclusion that he simply had had enough and had reached the stage where with his strong socialist principles he could not impose the hard medicine on the nation the economic turmoil demanded. Instead of being accused of bankrupting Britain, he decided to walk away and leave the mess for somebody else to deal with.

James Callaghan took-up the poisoned chalice and followed Harold Wilson into Downing Street and here again was a factor that could have totally changed the course of Britain's political and industrial history. Callaghan was a pleasant fellow with such a 'laid-back' attitude he was referred to as 'sunny Jim'. The Labour party had chosen him ahead of Dennis Healey, a tough uncompromising politician who opposed Arthur Scargill and his exorbitant wage demands. Healey had previously criticised the 'merry-go-round' of wage increases that was driving-up inflation. Had Healey been the Labour Party leader instead of Callaghan the head-on collision between government and miners that came later might have been averted. Within a few months sterling lost 13% of its value on foreign currency markets causing the government to have to borrow £5.5 billion to prop-up the currency, on top of previous heavy borrowings since 1974. By 1977 a government report claimed prices had increased 70% since Labour took over government.

As industrial unrest and relentless inflation continued to decimate the economy, nowhere was it felt more than in the Valley where the miners and their families had also to contend with the national bitterness against them for striking and trying to improve their miserable existence. Although it had been believed that a Labour government would fare better in dealing with the miners and the continuous assault on wages than a Tory government, it did not happen. A 'social contract' was negotiated by the government and the TUC to try to avoid the approaching economic chaos; to provide affordable wage increases and keep prices down, but the contract was continually under attack, particularly by the miners, and never achieved its objective.

When the miners submitted a demand for a wage of £135 a-week and a four day working week; Joe Gormley the President of the TUC and a former miner, appealed directly to the miners for restraint but without success. All sections of industry seemed to be taking it in turn to strike with even undertakers deciding on strike action. As the country went wearily into 1979 the strikes continued; railway workers, public servants, lorry drivers, dock workers steel and transport workers all combined to make a 'winter of discontent' the public would never forget.

The voters who had voted Labour back into power and to remove the discredited Edward Heath from office had also voted for peace and an end to violent confrontations, but it had not happened and in fact had worsened. James Callaghan's speeches denying Britain was sinking into chaos were heard in disbelief. Eventually Callaghan also caved-in, in much the same way Harold Wilson had surrendered and called a general-election he knew Labour was going to lose, but would enable him to walk away and leave the economic mess for the Tories to deal with.

Prime Minister Margaret Thatcher....

The people were in an unforgiving mood and returned the Tories to government with a substantial 70-seat majority. Almost immediately Margaret Thatcher, the new Prime Minister, outlined her plans to curb union power. The miners responded by rejecting a 20% wage increase and decided to take action to force the government into a 60% increase.

Margaret Thatcher set about rescuing the economy with great determination and made swinging public-spending cuts so that by 1981 the economy started to turn for the better in spite of continued strike action. Inflation was down to 15% and miraculously for the Tory government oil and gas had started to flow from the North Sea. On the downside, the NCB announced plans to close 23 pits but after threatened strike action the government withdrew the plans, preferring instead to wait and fight another day.

In 1982 unemployment had reached 3 million, mostly due to the massive cuts in public spending and services. The NCB in full knowledge of the government's total support offered the miners a wage increase of 9.3%, which to the fury of Arthur Scargill the NUM decided to accept in a national ballot.

By 1983, the economic tide was turning fast and the government rewarded the nation with a £2 billion cut in taxes. Margaret Thatcher was so popular that she won her second election with a massive majority of 188 seats and then immediately announced further cuts in public spending of £500 million. The Tory government was so successful and the economy improving so fast that the nation seemed impervious to unemployment having reached 3.3 million.

The government was fully aware that Arthur Scargill was determined to go for a national strike and had been making plans to store large stocks of coal and coke at power stations and steel works. Contingency plans were also made to ensure the police would be available in large numbers and had the equipment and resources to deal with violence. Dame Stella Rimington (MI5 Director General 1992 to 1996) published her auto biography in 2001 and revealed MI5 counter subversion exercises against the NUM and striking miners included the tapping of union leaders' telephones.

1984 – into the strike....

The NCB announced that an agreement reached with the NUM after the 1974 strike had become obsolete and that the NCB would go ahead with the closure of 23 uneconomic pits with the loss of 20 000 jobs. It seemed it was not considered by either the NCB or the government that closures of such magnitude would devastate large communities who depended almost entirely on the employment of their men at the local pits. There was no alternative employment in the Valley and miners would face years on the dole.

Scargill had been elected President of the National Union of Mineworkers (NUM) in 1981, but in 1982 the miners rejected his proposal to strike over pay. In October 1982, 61% of miners voted not to strike over pay and pit closures. He again called for a national strike in March 1983 and once again 61% of miners voted no. On the 1st March 1984 the NCB announced the closure of Cortonwood colliery at Brampton in the Valley, a colliery the NUM claimed still had many years of productivity left. The shock was immense in a tightly knit community that relied totally on the wages from the mine. The shock turned to anger at the way they were being treated after supplying the nation's energy over so many years. Following a local ballot, strike action started on the 5th March and within day's miners' pickets from the Yorkshire coalfield started picketing Nottinghamshire pits that were not threatened with pit closures and had decided not to support the strike. Arthur Scargill, President of the NUM declared that the strikes in all the coalfields were to be a national strike and called on all NUM members to support the strike. On the 8th March the Scargill led NUM national executive endorsed the decision of the Yorkshire and Scottish areas to strike without a national ballot taking place, but the Nottinghamshire, Northumberland and Leicestershire miners decided not to strike without a national ballot.

However, the strike was declared illegal as the NUM had not balloted all NUM members on the decision to strike; subsequently the courts ordered the confiscation of all NUM funds and assets. The ruling also enabled police to assist strike-breakers going into their place of work. This led to massive violence particularly in South Yorkshire and Nottinghamshire.

The strike was observed in the Yorkshire, South Wales and Kent coalfields, but the Nottinghamshire and Midlands coalfields that were not under threat of closure because of their large coal reserves and modern mining equipment refused to strike without a ballot. After being accused of being strike breakers, the Nottinghamshire miners decided to break away from the National Union of Mineworkers and formed the Union of Democratic Mineworkers that also attracted support from other regions.

Scargill had no option but to picket the Nottinghamshire pits because if they stayed open and supplied coal to power stations and industry it would undermine the national strike. The government then brought its prepared plans into action and flooded the Nottinghamshire coalfield with over 10 000 policemen to deal with the pickets that were intimidating and causing violence against the miners who wanted to work. Action by the police was brutal and it was claimed they terrorised the striking miners, arresting over 11 000 and charging over 8500 with offences. The Chief Constable of Manchester, John Anderton said, "The police are getting the image of a heavy handed mob". A statement that resonated with the miners claims that soldiers of the British Army were dressed in police uniforms for action against the miners. The claims probably had some credence when considering that police-forces throughout the country would have to have been stripped bare to provide the large numbers sent to Nottinghamshire.

Meanwhile the striking miners at Cortonwood set up their camp blocking access to the mine day and night. They were well supported by the local community in the Valley who contributed large quantities of soup and bread to sustain them, with some supporters supplying hot beverages and cigarettes.

The battle for Orgreave....

The struggle then moved on to the British Steel coking plant at Orgreave, South Yorkshire. British Steel's plants at Redcar and Scunthorpe would have had to close in less than two weeks if supplies of coal and coke were not delivered. The plants at Port Talbot, Ravenscraig and Llanwern had only stocks to last four weeks.

Arthur Scargill organised a mass picket at Orgreave of 6000 striking miners for the 18th June with the intention of blockading the plant and forcing closure. However, the government had been alerted to his plans through infiltration by MI5 and immediately brought counter measures into action, deploying 8000 policemen, 50 mounted police and 60 police dogs and handlers. No female police-officers were on duty although there were many women protesting among the strikers.

The police formed a line outside the plant facing the pickets and as numbers continued to increase on both sides the tension began to increase. When the miners started throwing stones the police used long-shields to protect their line. One policeman was hit in the face with a brick and was pulled out of the line. When trucks arrived to collect coke, the miners pushed forward attempting to break the police line causing the officer commanding the police to order a mounted charge. The miners quickly retreated and the mounted police returned to the rear of the police line. Another push forward by the miners was met with another mounted police charge and again the miners retreated. When stone throwing started again the police commander warned the miners that if they did not move 100 yards back away from the police line he would order short-shield squads to be used. (Short-shields are police in protective riot gear with batons and are used as an offensive rather than a defensive tactic in riot control). The miners refused to move back so the police launched a mounted charge with short-shield squads in pursuit causing panic among the miners with many beaten to the ground and arrested. Just after 9am fully laden trucks started to leave the plant causing the miners to push forward but the police forced them back enabling the trucks to pass.

After a lull in confrontation, some pickets rolled a tyre down a hill towards the police line and stone throwing started again. Short-shield squads took up positions and as they moved forward started to beat their shields with their batons, increasing the already tense atmosphere. The squads moved forward in a solid line and this time they didn't stop and kept advancing causing the miners who were outnumbered to retreat and try to escape across a railway line. Some of them escaped but others didn't and tried to fight back but they were no match against specially trained short-shield squads who brutally battered them to the ground and made many arrests.

After more short-shield charges during which Arthur Scargill was injured, a heavily supported police-line advanced forcing the miners to retreat into Orgreave village where they then formed a new line in Highfield Lane. The pickets continued to confront the police-line with hails of stones causing the police to make another mounted charge with short-shield squads pursuing and beating the miners.

The police eventually withdrew from the village and returned to their original police-line outside the plant, while the pickets built barricades with materials from a nearby scrap yard as protection from further mounted charges. By mid-afternoon the confrontation came to a stop, almost as by agreement, as both sides seemed too exhausted to continue. The police were particularly weary after suffering the summer heat in their thick blue uniforms and heavy riot gear. Casualties on both sides had been heavy with 72 policemen and 51 miners injured, although it is believed the number of miners injured was considerably more as many refused to go to hospital for fear of arrest. A further 97 miners who had been pursued by short-shield squads were brutally assaulted, knocked to the ground and arrested.

Betrayal....

Next day, the battle to close the Orgreave plant for which the miners had fought so hard was sabotaged by the Yorkshire NUM Executive who turned their back on the Orgreave struggle and instead sent the pickets back to Nottinghamshire. The precipitous decision by the Yorkshire Miners' leaders could well have been the turning point of the strike. The police were exhausted and it was questionable how much longer they could have continued with their tactics, while as miners were being arrested and injured many others were taking their place. Public opinion was also turning against the police as they witnessed horrific scenes on television of miners being charged by mounted police and the brutality of the short-shield squads clubbing fallen miners on the ground. Another day or two could have produced a totally different result.

Problems started mounting for Margaret Thatcher when a threatened rail strike was only narrowly averted when she personally intervened to increase a pay offer to rail workers. Another threatened strike by dock workers was only called off after the intervention and assistance from union leaders. Thatcher was fully aware she could only beat the miners if other unions could be kept on-side which became one of her major priorities. It also helped that many union leaders in the TUC had no love for Arthur Scargill and would be happy to see him fail, even if that meant propping-up a Tory prime Minister.

As the strike continued, the suffering of miners and their families in the Valley worsened but they showed great determination in the face of hunger, police intimidation and lack of support from social services. Members of other unions and public organisations organised donations of food to support the families as the miners struggled on through the cold winter months.

Beaten but defiant....

Finally, on the 3rd March 1985 the strike was called off. Miners unable to watch their suffering families any longer had started to slowly return to work and within a week a few had turned into a flood. The NUM executive voted to end the strike by only a small margin, but without any agreement on closures with the NCB.

Neil Kinnock, the leader of the Labour Party, criticised Arthur Scargill for the mess the miners were in. It could however be argued that it was the failure of the Labour Party and the TUC who failed to produce the socialist solidarity that could have saved the miners from defeat and the tragic consequences of the subsequent mine closures. Whatever the arguments, there was no doubt the Tories had been planning to defeat the miners ever since the miners' strike of 1974 and the humiliation of Edward Heath. Margaret Thatcher knew that if she could beat the miners then the bitter union disputes of the past would not occur again. Her objective had not just been to defeat the miners but also to destroy the power of the trade unions and this she achieved, but at a terrible cost to the nation.

After the strike....

Throughout the year long strike the miners had been surviving only on a small amount of NUM strike pay and were heavily in debt having not being able to pay rent, payments on cars and household goods. Many suffered the indignity of watching debt collectors invade their homes and carry away valuable and essential possessions. Others had to make beds on the floor for their children after bedroom furniture had been taken away. Most families had no TV's or radios and even children's toys were taken away as anything of value was claimed by debt collectors and bailiffs.

As the pit closures started at a fast rate after the strike, unemployment in the Valley was over 50%. Some miners with a better education or technical skills had to leave the Valley and the towns and villages of their birth to seek employment elsewhere, leaving once thriving communities with empty houses and closed shops. The health and depression problems of unemployed miners and their families became acute causing the suicide rate to increase significantly. The bitter hatred between those who supported the strike and those who had not never went away; dividing families and destroying the strong community spirit that had previously bound them together through all the bad times.

Arthur Scargill led over 200 000 men into the strike.

Over 20 000 were injured or hospitalised.

Two miners were killed on the picket line.

Two hundred served time in custody.

960 miners were sacked.

Thatcher planned revenge on the miners....

Winston Churchill had once declared the miners to be 'the enemy' and after Edward Heath's ignominious defeat by the miners, they were still considered by Margaret Thatcher to be 'the enemy' whom she was determined to defeat. It follows that with her hate of the miners that it was also the people of South Yorkshire, Kent, South Wales and Scotland who were the enemy and that she was declaring a class-war on fellow British men and women. The Tory government and the NCB had been secretly stockpiling massive reserves of coal and coke for over a year in the eventuality of a strike.

Additionally the government had been organising and training over 10 000 policemen in planned military operations, mostly drawn from the southern counties of England, who were given huge resources of equipment needed to meet violent confrontations.

Transport resources were also organised to give the police instant mobility to outpace flying pickets that Scargill had used successful in 1972. It was also strongly believed that the government had invested heavily in intelligence operations that had successfully infiltrated Scargill's top command structure that enabled the police to neutralise the effectiveness of flying pickets and planned demonstrations.

Although Margaret Thatcher and her government had planned over a long period to defeat the miners, no plans had made to deal with the massive unemployment and social deprivation that was to follow. The gloating over their victory over the miners and the revenge on Arthur Scargill for his defeat of Edward Heath was so intense that any thoughts of humanity for the suffering of the thousands of families as the mines started to close was never given any consideration.

Instead of condemnation for Thatcher betraying the working-class in the mining areas so severely; she was instead praised as a national hero and later claimed to be the architect of an economic miracle. But her victory was never complete, as her betrayal of the working-class created an even greater class division that has politically and socially divided Britain and could make it even more difficult for the Tories to achieve the national political dominance they had experienced in the Thatcher years.

It is a sad fact that after nearly three decade since the miners' strike the nation is increasingly divided. Repeated attempts by leading Tories to reduce the amount of unemployment benefits payable to the unemployed in the north of England while retaining a higher level in the south, illustrates the inbred antipathy that is still felt against former miners and their children, many of whom are also unemployed.

It is also a sad fact that the areas of the nation that provided the industry that created the massive wealth of the industrial revolution that found its way mostly south, has never received the assistance needed to regenerate what were some of the finest and most beautiful areas of the nation.

If Scargill had beaten Thatcher....

There are still many who believe that if Scargill had beaten Thatcher in the same way he brought down Edward Heath's government, that Britain would have been facing the prospect of a violent conflict and even civil-war. Scargill was known to have strong communist leanings and involvement with communist nations, but so did many others in the Labour Party and the unions. If it was ever Scargill's and the miner's intentions to turn Britain into a communist state, it was never made clear and such accusations usually came from the right-wing press.

What is known is that many senior members of the Labour Party and union leaders were in the pockets of the communist party; controlled and even financed with only one objective in mind which was to create a communist state in Britain. As Scargill's status increased he became a threat to the potential communist leadership in waiting who were desperate to stop him usurping their leadership.

Had Scargill defeated Thatcher, then almost certainly the pit closure programme would have been stopped, and it was believed by many, would have become such a severe strain on the economy that it could even have had a damaging effect on social spending and pensions. What has never been considered is that Scargill was convinced that there was still a big future for Britain's mining industry and that instead of closing mines the government should have been investing in further development. The cost of producing coal in Britain at the time was more expensive than importing cheap coal from overseas simply because the industry's production was too small to make it economical, while higher production that could have been mined from many long-life pits would have substantially reduced costs in the industry.

It also needs to be considered that at the time Thatcher was in the throes of an oil rush from the North Sea that gave her the opportunity to sort out of the miners (the enemy) once and for all. But now the oil is almost finished and Britain is being forced to build a nuclear energy industry that few Briton's really want and which is going to force the price of energy so high that few people in the working-class will be able to afford.

Arthur Scargill, for all his faults, always believed the coal industry held the key to Britain's future energy needs. Unfortunately, too many remember the terrible by-products of coal on the health of the nation; with millions of chimney pots, power-stations and steam engines spouting pollution and poisoning the air we breathed with devastating health consequences. Because of this coal has such a bad name that many cannot come to terms with its continued use. Yet it is known that Britain still has massive reserves of coal that could supply all the energy needs for the nation for the next 200 years with even more massive reserves under the North Sea; 'Mother Nature' pointing the way to rescue Britain from the economic tyranny of oil and gas but strangely ignored by political leaders still under the misguided antipathy of Churchill and Thatcher..

Many unsuccessful attempts have been made to explain the benefits of clean coal technology, that with further financial investment by the government in developing the technology further, would enable coal to be burnt safely without causing pollution and would be the answer to all Britain's energy needs. Yet both Labour and Tory governments are prepared to spend billions in subsiding nuclear energy provided by foreign firms and wind-farms despoiling the coast and countryside, when it is known that the investment of just £1 billion in developing clean-coal technology would be the answer to Britain's energy needs for the next two hundred years and far beyond.

Should Britain ever come to the realisation that clean-coal-technology could be Britain's economic salvation; the spin off in the export of the technology would create a massive surge in industrial exports that would also go a long way in vastly reducing pollution in countries such as China, India and South Africa who are totally reliable on coal produced energy.

Perhaps if Arthur Scargill had defeated Margaret Thatcher, the coal industry would have survived and the energy needs for the future would have been secured. Few will be prepared to give him any credit for the stand he took to help the coal industry to survive. With the further development of clean-coal technology and the revival of a coal industry, millions of unemployed in some of the poorest regions of Britain could be employed with massive savings in unemployment benefits and the regeneration of many of the depressed areas of Britain. My Valley and many other former mining areas would see such a resurgence that would propel them back into an era of national acceptance and employment that was viciously shorn from them by a vindictive Margaret Thatcher and an uncaring Tory Party troughing in wealth and privilege.

After Thatcher....

The disaster of Margaret Thatcher's and the Tories destruction of the mining communities has been well recorded, but sadly provoked little sympathy for the miners who are still even today regarded as 'the enemy'. But the bitterness of the people in the Valley has not gone away and remains a thorn in the Tory Party's attempts to obtain working majorities in government.

Life still continued to be a struggle for the Valley people, even after Thatcher met her just deserts. But proud and committed communities pulled together and in spite of many obstacles started to build a new life with what little they had been left with.

A massive Labour Party victory in 1997 brought in Tony Blair and a New Labour government and new hope in the Valley that at last they had their own government and that the darkness that had shrouded the Valley for so many years would at last be lifted. But it didn't happen. What started with many promises and good intentions soon dissolved into historic incompetence, greed and sleaze and became a government with little moral compass. As the Labour years passed, people in the Valley and the many other areas decimated with unemployment and hopelessness realised that they were being betrayed by their own Party and fellow socialists.

It would be wrong to taint the dedication of many of the Labour Party's MP's who fought long and hard battles in their attempts to keep the Party on a moral and socialist path, but as the Party degenerated in much the same way as previous Labour governments, their task to date became impossible.

Labour Party history....repeats itself....

History often repeats itself and in the history of the Labour Party, the many mistakes made by the Labour Party in the 1920's in allowing gentleman socialists such as Ramsay MacDonald to gain control of the Party has been repeated over the past two decades as traditional parliamentary working-class seats were continually hijacked by the Party elite. Many favoured and highly educated youngsters with little work or life experience have been parachuted into safe working-class seats. The practice by the Party hierarchy and elite of selecting candidates and ignoring the wishes of local Labour constituencies has operated to the disadvantage of working-class men and women being able to represent their people. Many younger members of the Party have been elevated to top positions in parliament with little or no experience of life at the coal-face and are unable to advance the socialist principles and ambitions of the vast working-class.

It would seem that it is now impossible for a genuine working-class man or woman to be selected as a potential Labour MP. Candidates without support from the elite or who do not have strong family connections in the Party, do not possess a good university degree or attended an elite school, have little chance of selection. Representation by the working-class in parliament has been almost eliminated by the powerful, greedy elite who use the Labour Party in much the same way as Ramsay MacDonald and only as a means to further their own ambitions and lust for power. The folly of this by the Party is reflected in the record of two of the most outstanding Valley Labour parliamentarians in Labour's recent history; Lord Mason of Barnsley and the 'Beast of Bolsover' Dennis Skinner MP.

Labour's outstanding parliamentarians....

Roy Mason, Baron Mason of Barnsley PC, a former coalminer, started his working life down a local mine in the Valley at the age of fourteen and became a National Union of Mineworkers official (NUM) in his mid-twenties. Mason won the Barnsley parliamentary seat at a by-election in 1953 and went on to serve the constituency for 40 years. Lord Mason was not an educated man but he did gain entrance to the LSE as a mature student on a TUC scholarship. During his remarkable career he served in Labour governments as Postmaster-General, Minister of State for Power, President of the Board of Trade, Secretary of State for Defence and Secretary of State for Northern Ireland. He is still today regarded as the most successful Cabinet minister to have served as Secretary for Northern Ireland. When Labour was defeated in 1979, the Tory Energy Secretary Nigel Lawson, advised the new Prime Minister Margaret Thatcher to appoint Mason the next Coal Board chairman, but Thatcher refused saying that "he is not one of us". A grave mistake by a bigoted Tory Margaret Thatcher, and how different the history of the miners' strike and industrial relations could have been had she had the courage to take Nigel Lawson's advice.

Dennis Skinner MP, passed his eleven-plus one year early, but went from grammar school to work down the mines. He went on to serve as leader of the Derbyshire NUM and also as a councillor and county councillor and attended Ruskin College when in his 30's. He was elected MP for the safe seat of Bolsover in 1970 and has held the seat ever since. Although Dennis is a far from articulate man he wears his left-wing credentials with pride and makes no apology for having supported Arthur Scargill during the miners' strikes when others such as Neil Kinnock and the TUC did not. Dennis Skinner's integrity, honesty and Party loyalty should be an example to the many errant Labour MP's and the Party leadership. He is one of the few Labour MP's who doesn't use the House of Commons subsidised bars and continually records one of the lowest claims for MP's Commons expenses. What a tragedy some Labour MP's have not been able to follow his exemplary personal and parliamentary record.

My Valley....

As the dark clouds still gather over my Valley today, all the signs of once thriving mining communities have almost disappeared, replaced instead with museums and local heritage sites. Just as before, the communities try to work together to make a better life and to give hope to their children and young people who witness the ever growing gap between their own lives and those who live in the more prosperous areas of the south. Many stout-hearted Labour councillors and Party supporters still strive to make a better life for their communities, but their efforts are largely negated by watching helplessly as their parliamentary constituency seats are stolen by the uncaring and selfish Labour Party elite.

Many of us in the Valley have travelled a long way since Clement Atlee regained government for the people and brought hope for a better future for our families. Some have managed to make a success of their lives in spite of all the social obstacles, but all too many are still trapped in a social environment fit only for 'the enemy' as decreed by Winston Churchill and Margaret Thatcher.

Perhaps the darkness will only be lifted when the Valley has the courage to break with a Labour Party that has lost its way, and when perhaps a leader will emerge who will reform the politics of the Valley and lead the Valley out of the dark and help the former mining communities to gain an equal and respected place in the national society whose wealth and success it helped to create, before it's too late.

Peter Hargreaves, Winchester.
2013.

The author....

Peter Hargreaves was born in the coal mining town of Wombwell in the heart of the Dearne Valley in South Yorkshire on the 8th December 1935. He is the third youngest in a family of thirteen children; the two eldest died as a result of malnutrition caused by the severe hunger and suffering inflicted on miners' families during the 1926 strike. The family lived in a two-up two-down terrace house with an attic and a coal cellar. Peter's father was foreman in charge of the colliery's huge coal fired boilers that made the steam to drive cages carrying men and coal up and down the pit shafts.

Leaving Secondary Modern School at the age of fifteen, where he had been top of his class and head prefect, he was destined to follow his brothers and spend his working life at the colliery, but fortunately due to new rules instituted after the coal industry was nationalised by the Atlee government, he was medically examined and found to be too small to do heavy work underground. Instead he was given work on the pit-top screens where he had to stand at a conveyor belt for eight hours a shift in clouds of coal dust hand sorting dross from coal.

He was later selected to work as a cleaner in the engine-room where the massive pistons drove the cages up and down the pit shaft. After just one year he was interviewed and selected to work in the colliery Landsale Office where he was employed until called-up for National Service.

Military service was with the West Riding infantry regiment the 1st Bn The Duke of Wellington's Regiment and saw service on the Rock of Gibraltar.

After national service he was recruited into the Lipton Limited retail group as a trainee manager and quickly progressed to be the company's youngest store manager at the age of 24. He was later responsible for developing the company's supermarket business and at the age of 28 was appointed executive in charge of the company's northern supermarkets.

Peter's first entry into politics was in 1965; standing as an Independent he broke an 18-year Labour Party monopoly of Wombwell Urban District Council. After joining the Liberal Party in 1969 he served as an Urban District and Metropolitan District councillor for fifteen years, during which time he was the Liberal Party candidate for the former Dearne Valley constituency at three general-elections during the turbulent 1970's.

Leaving for South Africa with his family in 1980 he was employed in several senior positions in the retail industry before being appointed Regional General Manager of Fraser's International (Swaziland) Limited and appointed to the board of directors.

After retiring in 2000 he returned to the UK in 2003 to reside with his family in Winchester and now writes books mostly on politics and current affairs.

Also by the author....

From the shop floor.
Stories you can only read in this book.
Thabo Mbeki – the dark side.
South Africa....a 'Terrible Silence'
(Nelson Mandela – Saint or sinner)
If Britain is broken – who broke it?
The men who broke Britain.
Betrayal....How the Labour Party betrayed Britain....
....and how the unions betrayed the Labour Party.

Printed in Great Britain
by Amazon